NAHUM

Readings: A New Biblical Commentary
A Trauma Bible Commentary

The Tomb of Nahum in Al-Qosh, Iraq,
after its destruction by the ISIS-militia in 2014
https://www.biblicalarchaeology.org/wp-content/uploads/2018/07/
al-Qosh-biblical-prophet-nahum-shrine.jpg

NAHUM

A Trauma for a Trauma

Bob Becking

SHEFFIELD PHOENIX PRESS
2024

Copyright © 2024 Sheffield Phoenix Press
Published by Sheffield Phoenix Press
University of Sheffield, S10 2TN

www.sheffieldphoenix.com

All rights reserved.
No part of this publication may be reproduced or transmitted in any form or by any means, electronic or mechanical, including photocopying, recording or any information storage or retrieval system, without the publisher's permission in writing.

A CIP catalogue record for this book
is available from the British Library

Typeset by the HK Scriptorium

ISBN: 978-1-914490-45-3 (HB)
ISBN: 978-1-914490-46-0 (PB)

To Jona, our grandson
Born nine/eleven 2022
That he may grow up in a peaceful world
And live without trauma

Contents

Abbreviations	ix
Preface	xiii
1. The Unceasing Trauma	1
2. Trauma Negated (the *Pax Assyriaca* Ideology)	13
3. Trauma Experienced (the 'Reality')	32
4. Trauma Continued (the History of Humankind)	52
5. The Book of Nahum: Composition and Date	55
6. Trauma for a Trauma: The Fate of Assyria and its Problems	79
7. Divine Duality and the Duel in History	103
8. The (Im)Morality of 'an Eye for an Eye'	113
Bibliography	120
Index of References	144

Abbreviations

AASOR	Annual of the American Schools of Oriental Research
AB	Anchor Bible
ABG	Arbeiten zur Bibel und ihrer Geschichte
ABL	Assyrian and Babylonian Letters Belonging to the Kouyunjik Collection of the British Museum
ADD	Assyrian Deeds and Documents
ADPV	Abhandlungen des Deutschen Palästina-Vereins
AfO	*Archiv für Orientforschung*
ANEM	Ancient Near Eastern Monographs
Ann.	Annals
AOAT	Alter Orient und Altes Testament
ARM	Archives royales de Mari
AsSt	Assyriological Studies
ATD	Das Alte Testament Deutsch
AYB	Anchor Yale Bible
BASOR	*Bulletin of the American Schools of Oriental Research*
BeO	Bibbia e Oriente
BEvTh	Beiträge zur evangelischen Theologie
BibOr	Biblica et orientalia
BIS	Biblical Interpretation Series
BiThSt	Biblisch-Theologische Studiesn
BKAT	Biblischer Kommentar. Altes Testament
BM	Texts in the British Museum (with collection number)
BN	*Biblische Notizen*
BWANT	Beiträge zur Wissenschaft von Alten und Neuen Testament
BZAbR	Beihefte zur Zeitschrift für altorientalische und biblische Rechtgeschichte
BZAW	Beihefte zur Zeitschrift für die alttestamentliche Wissenschaft
CAD	*The Assyrian Dictionary of the Oriental Institute of the University of Chicago*
CB OT	Coniectanea Biblica, Old Testament
CBETh	Contributions to Biblical Exegesis and Theology
CBQ	*Catholic Biblical Quarterly*

CeO	Classica et Orientalia
CHANE	Culture and History of the Ancient Near East
COS	*The Context of Scripture*
CT	Cuneiform Texts from Babylonian Tablets in the British Museum
CTN	Cuneiform Texts from Nimrud
DCH	*Dictionary of Classical Hebrew*
FRLANT	Forschungen zur Religion und Literatur des Alten und Neuen Testaments
HAE	Handbuch der althebräischen Epigraphik
HAR	*Hebrew Annual Review*
HBS	History of Biblical Studies
HSM	Harvard Semitic Monographs
HSS	Harvard Semitic Studies
HThKAT	Herder theologischer Kommentar zum Neuen Testament
IECOT	International Exegetical Commentary on the Old Testament
IEJ	*Israel Exploration Journal*
JANES	*Journal of the Ancient Near Eastern Society*
JAOS	*Journal of the American Oriental Society*
JBL	*Journal of Biblical Literature*
JEOL	*Jahrbericht van het Vooraziatisch-Egyptisch Gezelschap. Ex oriente lux*
JESHO	*Journal of the Economic and Social History of the Orient*
JESOT	*Journal for the Evangelical Study of the Old Testament*
JHS	*Journal of Hellenic Studies*
JNES	*Journal of Near Eastern Studies*
JNSL	*Journal of Northwest Semitic Languages*
JSOTSup	Supplements to the Journal for the Study of the Old Testament
KAI	*Kanaanäische und aramäische Inschriften*
KAT	Kommentar zum Alten Testament
KTU	*Die keilalphabetischen Texte aus Ugarit*
LHB/OTS	Library of Hebrew Bible/Old Testament Studies
ND	Texts from the excavations at Nimrud (with collection number)
NEB	Die Neue-Echter Bibel
NICOT	New International Commentary on the Old Testament
OBO	Orbis Biblicus et Orientalis
OIP	Oriental Institute Publications
ORA	Orientalische Religionen in der Antike
OTE	*Old Testament Essays*

OTL	Old Testament Library
OTS	Oud Testamentische Studiën
PEQ	*Palestine Exploration Quarterly*
PIA	Publications of the Institute of Archaeology
RA	*Revue d'assyriologie et d'archéologie orientale*
RINAP	Royal Inscriptions of the Neo-Assyrian Period
Rm.	Assurbanipal Rassam Cylinder
SAA	State Archives of Assyria
SAAB	*State Archives of Assyria Bulletin*
SAAS	State Archives of Assyria Studies
SBS	Stuttgarter Bibelstudien
SBTh	Studies in Biblical Theology
SHANE	Studies in the History of the Ancient Near East
SHCANE	Studies in the History and Culture of the Ancient Near East
SJOT	*Scandinavian Journal of the Old Testament*
SSN	Studia semitica neerlandica
StAT	Studien zu den Assur-Texten
TADAE	*Textbook of Aramaic Documents from Ancient Egypt*
TCS	Texts from Cuneiform Sources
ThW	Theologische Wissenschaft
UF	*Ugarit-Forschungen*
UM	Tablets in the collection of the University Museum of the University of Pennsylvania, Philadelphia
VT	*Vetus Testamentum*
VTE	Vassal Treaties of Esarhaddon (D.J. Wiseman)
VTSup	Supplementa to *Vetus Testamentum*
VWGTh	Veröffentlichungen der Wissenschaftlichen Gesellschaft für Theologie
WdO	Die Welt des Orients
WMANT	Wissenschaftlicher Monographien zum Alten und Neuen Testament
WUNT	Wissenschaftliche Untersuchungen zum Neuen Testament
ZA	*Zeitschrift für Assyriologie*
ZabR	*Zeitschrift für altorientalische und biblische Rechtsgeschichte*
ZAW	*Zeitschrift für die alttestamentliche Wissenschaft*
ZDPV	*Zeitschrift des deutschen Palästina-Vereins*

Preface

In 1957 my father died of cancer. Being a child of only six years old, I did not then understand the effect and consequences this event would have on my life. In those days, children were not supposed to grieve, but to go on with their life. Many years later, I started to realize the full impact of this bereavement. Writing a biography on the life of my father together with my two sisters was a comforting as well as a confronting experience (see Becking, Becking and Becking 2018).

In the early spring of 2020 the world was startled by the spread of the Covid-19 pandemic. Due to this virus and its mutations, millions of people got seriously ill, and too many died. Hundreds of thousands of people were thrown back into solitude and loneliness. Politicians were struggling to find a balance between the various interests and only laboriously found a path to a better future. On February 22, 2022, the Russian army invaded the independent republic of Ukraine, which led to a horrible war with too many civilians dying, too many lives wrecked, and too many soldiers traumatized.

All these events have made me sensitive for the devastating role that trauma—of whatever origin and character—plays in the life of human beings. I also realized that trauma is a perennial problem of humankind and that literary texts—from the dawn of civilization up to the present day—reflect the fissures that have been imprinted on us (see Garber 2015; Frechette and Boase 2016: 10-12; Huber 2020; Huber 2023; Watters et al. 2023). In this connection, I am thinking about the way in which the Gilgamesh depicts the struggle for acceptance of the constraints and boundaries of human life (George 2003; Zhu and Zheng 2020; De Villiers 2020) and the representation of trauma in the ego document of Katherine May (2020).

In the summer and autumn of 1976, I wrote my *doctoraalscriptie* (MSc-thesis) for the Faculty of Theology of Utrecht University on the book of Nahum arguing that this small prophetic book was a literary and conceptual coherent text (Becking 1977). Throughout my academic life I returned to the three chapters of this prophetic book, its beautiful poetry, its appealing imagery, as well as its complex composition. These issues at the primary level of the text and the search for a coherent view on the discrepancies at the surface of the chapters disabled a wider view until I realized that the Book of Nahum could—or probably should—be read as a reflection to trauma.

While I was working on this book, our grandson Jona was born. May he grow up to be a dove of peace in times of trauma. To his future I dedicate this book.

The various dimensions of this book have been touched upon in a multitude of publications—more than the stars at night—on biblical studies, trauma studies, studies of the history of the Neo-Assyrian Empire, etc. It is impossible to quote each and every publication. I apologize to all those colleagues and friends who don't find themselves quoted.

1

The Unceasing Trauma

As have often been observed, the book of Nahum—like the book of Jonah—ends with a question:

> Over whom did not come your evil continually? (Nah. 3.19)

This concluding question evokes a few exegetical questions:

- To whom do the pronominal forms refer?
- Which people had suffered under the evil?
- Which person or nation was the source of this evil?
- Can anything be said about the character of this 'evil'?
- Can this 'evil' be classified as 'trauma'?

In my opinion, the answers to these questions need to be primarily sought in the literary context of the line in Nah. 3.19. In a second tier, the historical context might be helpful.

1.1 Who Suffered?

A first answer to this question can be found in the preceding line in Nahum that reads:

> All who hear the hearsay about you
> Will clap their hand on you. (Nah. 3.19)

The 'clapping of the hands' is a gesture of joy on the downfall of the city (see Fox 1995; Fabry 2006: 223-24; Hagedorn 2011: 63; see also Ps. 47.2). In this line the gesture expresses joy—for those who hear the news—as well as a wicked delight on the fate of those who brought the evil. Who were they? The text of Nah. 3.19 as such does not give an answer, but the book as a whole contains a few hints.

In connection with the noun 'hearsay', it should be remarked that twice in the book of Nahum, mention is made of messengers. The first attestation is in Nah. 2.1:

Look, there on the mountains,
    the feet of one who brings good news,
        who proclaims peace!
Celebrate your festivals, Judah,
    and fulfil your vows.
No more will the wicked invade you;
    He, in fact, will be completely destroyed.[1]

This verse introduces a clear message of hope for Judah. Those taken into exile will be liberated and invited to return joyfully to Jerusalem and surroundings. This message stands in sharp contrast to the remark on the fate of other messengers:

'I am against you',
    declares Yhwh of Hosts.
'and I will destruct her chariot into smoke,
    and the sword will devour your young lions.
        I will cut off from you your prey on earth.
The voice of your messengers will no longer be heard.' (Nah. 2.14)

These words form the final lines in a section containing a prophetic portrayal and poetic description of the—to the author impending—downfall of Nineveh.

This implies, in my opinion, that the noun $šēma‘$, 'hearsay', in Nah. 3.19 refers to the rumors and reports on the ruination of Nineveh. All (kol) who receive that message will burst out in joy. It can be deduced that these 'all' were those who had suffered. That is, however, not a definitive answer to the question posed.

How inclusive should 'all' be construed? There are, at first sight, three possibilities:

1. Only those within Judah who had suffered;
2. Only those within Judah who had suffered and those in exile;
3. All inhabitants of Judah;
4. All inhabitants of Judah as well as of the former Northern Kingdom;
5. All people who had suffered from the Neo-Assyrian Empire.

---

1. ET 2.1; I follow the order of the Hebrew Bible.

These possibilities show a change from particularism to inclusiveness. The text of the book of Nahum is not decisive on this point. In scholarship there is a tendency toward the fifth possibility mentioned (e.g. Rudolph 1975: 187; Van der Woude 1978: 126; Deissler 1984: 216; Renaud 1987: 320-21; Roberts 1991: 77; Bosman 2002: 359; Christensen 2009; Dietrich 2016: 85-86; Jeremias 2019: 210-11; Timmer 2020: 173-74; T. Renz 2021: 191). Petersen, for instance, states that no one could have escaped the Assyrian terror (2002: 199). He, however, leaves open the question whether or not this would include only Israelites. Van der Woude (1978: 126) clearly states that all Levantine states are implied. He argues for this position with a reference to the then recent history of Assyrian violence and humiliation. This position has two implications that will be discussed later on in this book. Van der Woude—and others—construe the Neo-Assyrian rule over Western Asia as an ongoing chain of crimes against humanity, and this way the book of Nahum is freed from the suspicion of being a particularistic Judah-centred document.

I am aware of the fact that some scholars assume this final line of the book to be a gloss (e.g. Jeremias 1970: 46; Schulz 1973: 102-103; Seybold 1989: 28-34, 66-67; Nogalski 1993b: 123-27; Spronk 1997: 144; Fabry 2006: 223; Wöhrle 2008: 44-52; Hagedorn 2011: 63-64). The arguments for this view that would deprive the book of Nahum of its more universalistic character are not strong. The fact that the final clauses would be in prose is not a redaction-historical argument (see Dietrich 2016: 86-88; Jeremias 2019: 210). The—as such incorrect—observation by Spronk that the other instance where the root ʿbr occurs in the book of Nahum (2.1) is part of a later redaction can be set aside as an example of circular reasoning.

1.2 Who Imposed the Suffering?

These deliberations already gave an answer to the second question. Both Nah. 2.9 and 3.7 mention the city of Nineveh ($nîn^e wēh$):

> Nineveh was like a pool of water during her days,
>   but now they are running away;
> 'Stop! Stop!'
>   But no one turns! (Nah. 2.9)

> Everyone who sees you will turn away from you in disgust;
>   they will say, 'Nineveh has been devastated!
> Who will lament for her?'
>   There will be no one to comfort you!' (Nah. 3.7)

Both verses are part of prophecies of doom directed against the Neo-Assyrian capital. In the book of Nahum a few glimpses are given on the view of the author with regard to the conduct of the Neo-Assyrians. In this perception, the Assyrian army is compared with a strong lion:

> The lion tore apart as much prey as his cubs needed
>   and strangled prey for his lionesses;
> he filled his holes with prey
>   and his dwelling places with torn flesh. (Nah. 2.13)

In a *woe*-oracle (on this genre see Westermann 1964: 137-42; Janzen 1972; Hillers 1984: 31), Nineveh is accused of being a liar and a greedy extortioner:

> Woe to the city of bloodshed!
>   all of lies;
> filled with plunder;
>   who does not stop to plunder. (Nah. 3.1)

1.3 The Character of the Evil

These observations hint at the character of the evil imposed, or better: the collective memory on the Assyrian conduct, or: the way the author of the book of Nahum wants the readers to assess this period. Before jumping to conclusions with regard to the character of the Assyrian rule, a few remarks must be made.

- The Hebrew noun *rāʿâ*, 'evil, harm, disaster, crime", is not a descriptive term, but an evaluative one (see Foster 2022). This means that the author of the book of Nahum is not presenting an objective report on the deeds and doings of the powerful empire, but is giving an assessment on that conduct. Presenting an event as 'evil' is implicitly or explicitly based on a normative worldview or religious conviction.[2]
- The Hebrew substantive *rāʿâ*, 'evil, harm, disaster, crime", like the adjective *rāʿ* has a broad specter of meaning. Clines (*DCH* VII, 521-25) distinguishes four major ways to turn the Hebrew noun into English (see below).
- It is a well-known fact that when it comes to the assessment of deeds and doings as trauma, the position of the person in connection with a certain

---

2. See the discussion in philosophical ethics on the 'is-ought problem' raised by David Hume in 1740: e.g. Schurz 1997; Chilovi and Wodak 2021.

action is of great importance. Someone who had acted upon someone else often has an inclination to downplay the dramatic effect or to hide behind the veil of excuses. Someone who has been acted upon could enhance the pain in describing the event. Bystanders often, but not always, take a neutral position or seek vindication for their lack of courage to intervene.

I will discuss these three problems.

1.3.1 Evaluative

This point seems to be self-evident. Words like 'evil' or 'trauma' are not just descriptive but always based on a moral code by which a person, a group or a society assesses an event. When it comes to communication of sentences like 'That car accident was traumatic' or 'The melting of the Arctic ice is an evil', the sender and the receiver of that message have to be sharing the underlying moral code. Otherwise, the communication would end in misunderstanding or alienation between the two parties involved. By implication, the assessment of the Neo-Assyrian occupation of Judah—and other former states—as 'evil' or 'traumatic' is in need of a clear and acceptable definition of the moral categories involved.

1.3.2 Fields of Meaning

What does the Hebrew substantive *rā'â* mean? The four areas identified by Clines are:

1. Moral evil. The noun is used in cases where the moral code of a society is trespassed. Two instances exemplarily clarify this notion. In the story on the sexual union of the sons of the gods with the daughters of men (Gen. 6.1-7) these acts of mingling and merger are qualified as transgressions of the moral boundary supposedly set between the realm of the divine and the worlds of humans:

> YHWH saw how great the wickedness (*rā'â*) of the human race had become on the earth, and that every inclination of the thoughts of the human heart was only evil all the time. (Gen. 6.5)

In the narrative on the sexual atrocities against the wife of the Levite from Bethlehem that took place in Gibea, the conduct of the villagers is twice classified as *rā'â*.

> Then the Israelites said, 'Tell us how this awful thing (*rā'â*) happened'. (Judg. 20.3)

And:

> The tribes of Israel sent messengers throughout the tribe of Benjamin, saying, 'What about this awful crime (*rāʻâ*) that was committed among you? (Judg. 20.12)

This moral verdict stands parallel to the qualification of the wrongdoers as 'sons of Belial' (Judg. 19.22). They were seen as breakers of the hospitality and sexual abusers.

2. Evil leading to harm, injury or mischief. In his answer to the request of Moses to let his people go and celebrate a religious festival in the desert, the Pharaoh of Egypt says:

> YHWH be with you—if I let you go, along with your women and children! Look out, there is mischief in front of you. (Exod. 10.10)

As an ironical note, the narrator has the Pharaoh utter his empathy with the Hebrews. He wants to avert that something bad will happen to them. An ostracon from Arad contains the at first sight enigmatic ending (Arad 40 = Arad (8):40: 14-15):

> [And th]is is the evil that Edo[m has done] (Renz 1995: 148)

Or:

> [... until] the evil that Edo[m devises dis]appears (Na'aman 2003a: 200)

I will not go into the details of the epistolary and historiographic context of this line. Suffice it for the argument here that *rʻh* in this inscription refers to a military attack of the Edomites on Judaean territory during the reign of Hezekiah (Na'aman 2003a). This attack is negatively assessed as an infringement of Judaean territory.

Psalm 38 is an emotional and evocative prayer of someone who in the midst of suffering asks for divine help. The illnesses and inflictions are brought upon him by his enemies who act instrumentally on God's behalf. Although the supplicant treats his enemies correctly:

> They repay me evil (*rāʻâ*)
>   for the good;
> they are inimical
>   to me following what is good. (Ps. 38.21)

In his text the poet assesses the wounds on his body and his soul as evil acts.

3. Evil as trouble, misfortune or misery. In this category all sorts of events characteristic for a broken creation or the busted life that can often not be connected to a clear source of harm bringing can be listed. A nice example is a line in Psalm 37:

> They will not be ashamed in the time of evil (*rā'â*);
> In the days of hunger they will be sated. (Ps. 37.19)

From the parallel with 'the days of hunger' it becomes clear 'the time of evil' will be an era of lack and despair. The context does not make clear by whom this dark period will be brought upon the 'blameless' (v. 18). Another example can be found in the book of Proverbs:

> A prudent one will see evil (*rā'â*)
>   and hide himself,
> but the simple-minded will pass by
>   and paid for it. (Prov. 22.3)

'Evil' has here an indistinct haziness to which human reaction is—at least—twofold. It should be noted that the expression *bô'* + *rā'â* + *'el*, 'to bring evil upon (someone)' is always clear about the identity of the person or deity who brought the misery. See for instance:

> Then Absalom and all the men of Israel said,
>   'The advice of Hushai the Arkite sounds better than the advice of Ahithophel'.
>   Now YHWH had ordained to frustrate the sound advice of Ahithophel, so that YHWH could bring a calamity (*rā'â*) on Absalom. (2 Sam. 17:14)

4. *Displeasure*. This fourth category is only found twice in the Hebrew Bible, once in a palaeo-Hebrew inscription and four times in the writings from Qumran. In the narrative of Jonah, the main character reacts baffled by the fact that YHWH reversed the prophecy of doom for the inhabitants of Nineveh:

> This displeased (*rā'â*) Jonah greatly and he became angry. (Jon. 4.1)

God's conversion after the conversion of the Ninevites made Jonah shake on the foundations of his existence. He became angry on God's kindness. A comparable idiom can be found in the book of Nehemiah. When the news on the mission of Nehemiah reached the leaders of Samaria:

> ... it was very displeasing (*rā'â*) to them that someone had come to seek the welfare of the sons of Israel. (Neh. 2.10)

Sanballat the Horonite and Tobiah the Ammonite were unpleasantly affected by this mission to restore Jerusalem, which might lead to an end of their political and religious privileges.

On the silver amulets excavated at Ketef Hinnom—presenting a variant text of the Priestly Blessing from Numbers 6—the noun $r'h$ occurs in a broken context:

1. [...] ? blesse[d]
2. [...]yahu
3. [...]yah[u]
4. [...] evil ($r'h$) [...]
5. [...] May bless you
6. Yahu and
7. [k]eep you.
   (Ketef Hinnom 2 = Jer. (x):35:1-7; see Renz 1995; for a different reading see Barkay, Vaughn, Lundberg and Zuckerman 2004)

Although this passage is full of riddles and uncertainties, the interpretation above suggests that the supplicant wishes that his or her misery will be removed by a divine act of blessing.

According to Clines (*DCH*, VII: 522), the word $rā'â$ in Nah. 3.19 should be interpreted as an example of the second category. The author of the book of Nahum then is seen as assessing the deeds and doings of the Neo-Assyrians as evil leading to harm for Judah and probably also other nations. I agree with a remark. Could it not be that at the same time the Neo-Assyrians were trespassing a line in the moral code? At a conceptual level, their conduct could be seen as a punishment of Israel for the sins of the people. But by abusing their mandate the Neo-Assyrians went beyond the expected. I will come back to this point in section 8.2. The exact character of the harm done can of course not be established merely by an analysis of the noun $rā'â$. Historical and archaeological evidence is needed. But first a warning must be made.

1.3.3 *Point of View and the Malleability of Memory*

The character of this warning becomes clear from an example regarding atrocities during the Great War—or First World War. After the invasion in Belgium and France in August 1914, soldiers from the German army perpetrated brutal atrocities. That the acts of execution of civilians by a firing squad and the rape of Belgian and French women really took place has long been fiercely discussed and debated. Especially from the German side the reports of the deaths of thousands of unarmed civilians have been construed as mere fabrications. They were seen as constructed by anti-German Allied propagandists in order to demonize the invaders. On the other hand, German propaganda on this period has been full of Belgian and French atrocities against German soldiers and citizens by para-military groups of *franc-tireurs*. Meticulous research in the archives of Belgium, Britain, France, Germany and Italy, however, has revealed a German campaign of brutality that led to the deaths of some 6,500 Belgian and French civilians.

The German claim that the civilians were guerrillas, executed for illegal resistance, turned out to originate in a vast collective delusion on the part of German soldiers. During the war, these reports nevertheless functioned as propaganda especially to draft neutral countries to take side in the conflict. After the war, the topic became part of a process of blaming the other and building the myth of the beastliness of the other party (see Horne and Kramer 2002; Buelens 2015).

This twentieth century CE example makes clear that texts and artifacts presenting the Neo-Assyrian conquest and occupation of Judah and other Levantine states should be treated carefully. They are biased by the point of view of their authors or sculptors as they represent the memory that had arisen on the 'other'.

I will mention a few examples of texts assessing the character of the Neo-Assyrian acts, one positive and one negative. (1) King Warikas (Urikki) of Que in Anatolia became a vassal of Tiglath-Pileser III. In a bilingual Luwian-Phoenician inscription he states that merging with the Assyrian Empire worked out in a positive way:

> ... I also acquired horse [upon horse and ar]my upon army. The king [*of Ashur and*] all the house of Ashur became for me a father [and] a mother. And Danunians and Assyrians became one house.
> (Çineköt Inscription: 6-10; see Tekoğlu and Lemaire 2000; Simon 2014; Novak and Fuchs 2021; *COS* 4.15 [Luwian] and 4.16 [Phoenician])

Being a vassal brought Warikas wealth and well-being. He felt accepted by the Assyrian court (see Lanfranchi 2009). (2) Quite a different image is found in an inscription by the Babylonian king Nabonidus:

> [The city] of Sennacherib, son of Sargon, offspring of a house slave, conqu[eror of Babylon], [plund]erer of Akkad, its roots I shall pluck out and the foundations of the land I shall obliterate. [The . . .] from his family forever from Assyria I shall exile. [Because] of the crimes against Akkad which you committed, Marduk, great lord, [and the great gods] shall call [you] to account
> (BM 55467 Rev. 7-11; ed. Gerardi 1986:36).

These lines give the impression that the Assyrian campaigns against Babylon were experienced as traumatic and were calling for revenge (see al-Rawi 1985; Cogan 2021: 158). The Neo-Assyrian kings, on the other hand, presented themselves as faithful instruments in the hands of their gods. See, for instance, a passage that often opens Sennacherib's Annals:

> Sennacherib, the great king,
> the mighty king, king of the universe, king of Assyria,
> king of the four quarters (of the earth); the wise shepherd,
> favorite of the great gods, guardian of the right,
> lover of justice; who lends support,
> who comes to the aid of the needy, who turns (his thoughts) to pious
>   deeds;
> perfect hero, mighty man;
> first among all princes, the powerful one who consumes
> the insubmissive, who strikes the wicked with the thunderbolt;
> the god Assur, the great mountain, an unrivaled kingship
> he has entrusted to me, and above all those
> who dwell in palaces, has made powerful my weapons
>   (e.g. Oriental Institute Prism I; Luckenbill 1924: 23; RINAP 3,1:1-4;
>   see Frahm 1997: 99-102)

This passage is exemplary for the Neo-Assyrian royal ideology in which conquests, devastations and exiles are not seen as evil acts but as expressions of the good shepherdship by the king (see, e.g., Liverani, Lemche and Pfoh 2021).

1.4 Was the Assyrian Occupation Traumatic?

An answer to this question depends on two other questions: first, how to define trauma and traumatic, and second, what evidence is there for the Neo Assyrian period? The first will be discussed below and the second in the next two chapters.

1.4.1 The Many Faces of Trauma

1.4.1.1 Medical

In medicine, the word 'trauma' refers to an injury that is seen as an interruption of the continuity of a tissue. All parts of the body can be touched or wounded due to the action of external influences, such as a hit, a fire, a car accident, a fall down the stairs, etc. By the phrase 'interruption of the continuity' of the skin, the bone, or any other part of the body is meant that the expected development of the organism is interrupted. There are of course degrees in the severity of a trauma depending on the force of the interruption. Most small traumas can easily be healed by medical treatment and will not lead to a traumatic aftermath. Sincere traumas, however, could lead to disability and even death. Such injuries could be the cause of a traumatic existence (see, e.g., Eastman, Rosenbaum and Thal 2008; Egol, Koval and Zuckerman 2010; Van der Kolk 2014; Huber 2020).

1.4.1.2 Psychological

Sincere bodily injury can lead to psychic trauma. In psychology, trauma is understood as an unresolved event from the past, such as an accident, death of an important person, sexual abuse or violence. Such a trauma can feel like an invisible wound in the soul. Such a trauma is invisible from the outside; nevertheless it hurts a person. The event continues to cause unpleasant and confusing emotions. The reliving of the event—often subconscious—or thinking about it a lot leads to anxiety. To avoid such anxiety the event is often silenced or dissimulated.

A trauma will be developed if the event has made such an impression on the person that it is difficult to accept it or locate it as a part of life. After a major injury people have to deal with different emotions such as fear, sadness, helplessness, guilt or anger. This is a natural reaction of the bodily system. Often these emotions will subside on their own. When, however, this is not the case and people continue to suffer, a trauma can be diagnosed.

The experience of something unpleasant and discomforting over an extended period or several times will develop multiple or complex trauma. Examples include recurrent assault, repeated sexual abuse, or being bullied over and over again. Because a person had to deal with the same trigger several times, the psychological complaints can be stacked in the case of a multiple or complex trauma. They will include for instance an anxiety disorder, a negative self-image or addiction problems. Multiple or complex trauma can affect the character of a person and development of life because the trauma has been absorbed 'deeper' into the system.

Everyone experiences the symptoms of trauma differently. In general, people often travel back to the situation over and over again without resolving the pain. Trauma makes it difficult to focus on reality. Trauma can be noticed in the body. The stress level of the body is increased, leading to a continuous state of alertness. At times, a trauma is accompanied by an increased heart rate and respiratory rate. Victims of trauma feel rushed for no apparent reason. The emotional complaints can also occur at any time of the day (see—among a hoard of publications—Herman 1997; Scaer 2014; Frechette and Boase 2016; Wenyi 2021: 26-48).

Treatment for this kind of trauma is a careful enterprise. A physician, psychotherapist, or a psychiatrist have various treatments at disposal: exposure therapy, cognitive therapy, EMDR, EFT and some others. Not every treatment works in a comparative way in different cases. Patience and diligence are needed.

1.4.1.3 Sociological
When a complete group or a part of a society is suffering from the aftermath of a severe disruption of the life and happiness of that group, we speak of a collective trauma. This form of trauma is characterized by something that not only disturbs individual lives but also distorts the fabric of a community in its entirety. The coherence and the elasticity of a group are violated and defamed, especially the supporting beams of the group identity. The collective sails adrift through the fog of sadness.

The history of humankind is overloaded with examples of collective trauma: the burden of the Hebrews in ancient Egypt (if historical), the disproportional violence of the crusaders, slavery in all its forms, the holocaust, 9/11, the Covid pandemic, etc. All these events left a burning mark on the identity and the delight in life of too many people. Groups and communities are continuously busy reinventing themselves (see Erikson 1976, 1995; Herman 1997; Alexander 2012; Frechette and Boase 2016; Wenyi 2021: 26-48).

There does not seem to be an accepted treatment for collective trauma. As far as I understand, the acceptance of what really happened and commemorations in public events can have a healing force. The salute to the fallen of the Great War at the Menin Gate in Ypres on Armistice Day (November 11) is a good example. The performing of the 'last post' is a moving act.

1.4.1.4
Different from 'evil', trauma is a relatively objective indication, although it has a subjective dimension, as indicated above. Trauma—in body, soul and community—is recognizable even behind the veils so often placed. Despite this perceptibility, it remains unfathomable to gauge what the real effect is for person, life, or future.

1.4.2 The Assyrian Occupation
Between the campaigns of Tiglath Pileser III to the west and the lost battle of Nineveh in 612 BCE (Zawadzki 1988), the Assyrians were lord and master of the territory of the Levant, that is, the coastal strip along the Mediterranean from Turkey to the border with Egypt. A greater part of this area consisted in Assyrian provinces; the other part in client kingdoms with a vassal status. Nahum 3.19 construes this period as full of evil acts. In the next chapters, I will discuss the question of what evidence there is for such acts and whether they can be labelled as traumatic for the inhabitants of that region. It should be noted that the sources available only show the outside of a trauma. Although they contain hints and signs of the trauma, the real impact on humans is difficult to fathom.

2

Trauma Negated
(the *Pax Assyriaca* Ideology)

2.1. 'It Will Be Okay: Everyone Has a Scar'

Too easily uttered and too often heard are pseudo-consoling words in front of experiences that can have a traumatic impact—sometimes with good intentions, but mostly to silence one's own fears and demons. People of all times and many places have tried to calm down the anxiety of persons in their immediate vicinity who are in shock by bad things that happened to them (Liem 2007). Persons receiving such superficial solace do not feel consoled, but abnegated. There could be listed a legion of examples from the friends of Job (see Van Loon 2018, esp. 133-209; Zhang 2020) up to the soothing words of present-day evangelical preachers (see Hall et al. 2020). They all have in common the denial of the depth of the injuries in body and soul.

With regard to the 'evil' mentioned in Nah. 3.19, two sets of ideas have been developed with the intention to soothe the hardship of the 'yoke of Assur': the ideology of the *pax assyriaca* and the view that the Assyrians did not impose their religion on the inhabitants of the province Samerina and the vassal state of Judah. They will now be presented.

2.2. *Pax Assyriaca*

2.2.1. The Proposal

The concept of the Assyrian peace has been developed on the basis of the idea of the *Pax Romana* (see Goldsworthy 2016; Cornwell 2017; Faust 2021: 238-48). The idea of an imperial Roman peace refers to the period in the

Roman Empire when the neighboring and rebellious countries were pacified and Rome's hegemonial grip led to prosperity—at least for the Romans and those who associated with them. The concept of the *pax assyriaca* assesses the situation in the Assyrian Empire after the period of conquest by Tiglath-Pileser III, Shalmaneser V, Sargon II and Sennacherib up to the first signs of the downfall of the empire (700–630 BCE). After 700, the Assyrians did not expand their empire except for a few campaigns to Egypt[1] that, however, did not lead to the incorporation of the land of the Nile in the Assyrian Empire on a more permanent base (see Kuhrt 1995: 499-500; Ruzicka 2012: 6-9; Kahn 2006). According to this view, the Assyrian interest in the area of Samaria, Judah and Philistia led to regional prosperity and wealth through the production of goods that could be transported to the core of the empire. The absence of war and the Assyrian incentives would have enhanced the local economy (Kuhrt 1995: 535-36). According to Otto (1999: 37-75), the concept of *pax assyriaca* is based in the Neo-Assyrian royal ideology. In this ideology the king is both a revenging conqueror and a shepherd for all the conquered people, aiming at their welfare and prosperity. The footprints of this Assyrian peace are believed to be seen in the following examples.

Excavations at Tel Miqne-Ekron have brought to light an almost industrial complex for the production of olive oil dating from the seventh century BCE (Gitin 1989). According to Seymour Gitin, the excavator, this complex was the result of the Neo-Assyrian interest in food production that provided the Assyrian core and at the same time provided prosperity for the region (Gitin 1989: 48; 1995; followed by Finkelstein and Singer-Avitz 2001: 253; Finkelstein, Gadot and Langgut 2022).

In the Negev, settlement expansions, especially in the Beersheba and Arad valleys, are clear signs from this region of prospering trade. It seems that cedar trees from the Lebanon were imported in great numbers. These findings are generally interpreted as the result of the *pax assyriaca*. The increased Arabian caravan trade through the Negev to the Philistine coast too furthered this economic revival (Na'aman 1987, 1995).

In Transjordan, the seventh century was a period of demographic growth for both the kingdom of Ammon and that of Edom. This blossoming of the region has generally been connected with the *pax assyriaca* and the impact of the trade routes from the Arab peninsula through this area—the Kings Road (Na'aman 1993, 1995; Finkelstein 1995: 137; Knauf 1995; Van de Mieroop 2007: 252-66).

---

1. Esarhaddon conquered Memphis in 671, see Esarhaddon Victory Stele from Sinjirli: Rev. 36-44; with, e.g., Spalinger 1974; Ashurbanipal conquered Thebes in 663; see Streck 1916, 16 = Rm. Col II:37-39, and 164 = Ann. 1:74.

These finds have reinforced the *pax assyriaca* thesis. According to this view, the Assyrian occupation of the southwestern Levant cannot be labelled as a form of suppression, but rather as a period of economic blossoming at the price of Assyrian overlordship. In this view, the statement in Nah. 3.19 is an exaggerated opinion from the point of view of the inhabitants of the conquered and pacified areas. In scholarly opinion, the *pax assyriaca*-paradigm is dominant (next to the authors mentioned in this section; Bunimovitz and Lederman 2003; Connan et al. 2006; Lanner 2006: 63-69; Fales 2020: 238-47; Gitin 2012; Younger 2015; Moriconi and Tucci 2015; Rede 2018; Toro 2022). The idea, however, has been challenged on good grounds, as will be elaborated in the next section.

2.2.2. Challenge and Criticism

Although the *pax assyriaca* thesis is widely accepted, scholars have questioned the theory. The absence of evidence for the assumption that the Assyrians would have initiated the trade in this region has been pointed out (Elat 1978: 27-28). The prosperity of the region—as exemplified in the olive industry at Ekron—has been attributed to a period of Egyptian hegemony over southern Israel (Stager 1996; criticized however by Gitin 2003). Na'aman has argued that there are no traces of a deliberate Neo-Assyrian strategy to bring the region into prosperity (Na'aman 2003b). It has been pointed out that the Neo-Assyrians had no interest in developing the economy in the newly established provinces. Their aim was to collect taxes for the royal coffers (see, e.g., Grayson 1995; Gitin 1995: 61; Schloen 2001: 146; Faust and Weiss 2005). Cogan (2021) has collected written and archaeological evidence on the harshness of the yoke of Assur both for the province of Samerina and the vassal state of Judah.[2]

In a very thorough and well-researched monograph, Avraham Faust has collected and analysed all available archaeological and written evidence that could shed light on the veracity of the *pax assyriaca* thesis (Faust 2021). It is impossible to summarize his book in a few paragraphs. I will therefore highlight four important issues.

1. Demographic developments. Although it is impossible to construct exact figures concerning the size of the populations in the southwestern end of the Assyrian Empire, comparative numbers and tendencies can be deduced from the archaeological data. The number of settlements in a specific area and the size (growing or waning) of the settlement can give a clear indication. Faust correctly argues that the demographic developments

---

2. They will be discussed in chapter 3 below.

differed between the newly established Assyrian provinces, for instance Samerina, and the vassal states with their client kings surrounding the area of the Assyrian Empire. While the evidence from the provinces displays a demographic decrease, the data form the client-states hint at an increase of the population (Faust 2008, 2015, 2021).

This remarkable fact can be explained as follows. On the one hand, the Assyrians deported greater parts of the population of the newly installed provinces. The hilly area around Samaria was not fit for the Assyrian agricultural production that was developed for the flat areas in Mesopotamia. The overland transport to the core of the empire would have been difficult and cost-ineffective. Therefore, the Assyrians deported many people from the conquered areas to have them till the soil in newly established agricultural areas in Mesopotamia to help feed the urbanizing core of the empire. On the other hand, it can be assumed that inhabitants from the former kingdom of Samaria sought refuge in Judah. There is, however, no hard evidence for this assumption.

The client kingdoms—Judah, the Philistines, Moab, Ammon, Edom—had to pay a yearly tribute to Assyria. This turned out to be an incentive for economic and hence demographic growth. It should be noted that this growth was enabled by the expanding Phoenician sea trade in the seventh century. Their network across the Mediterranean turned out to be very profitable, and the neighboring areas in the southern Levant got a piece of the pie (see Faust 2021).

2. Economic growth. In the Assyrian province of Samerina there are no signs of economic blossoming, quite the contrary. In the Neo-Assyrian Nimrud Prism a *narratio* on the conquest by Sargon II of Samaria is found (Nimrud Prism IV: 25-41; see Gadd 1954):

25. [The inhabitants of Sa]merina, who 28) agreed 25) with a king
26. [hostile (?) to] me not to endure servitude
27. [and not to br]ing tribute
28. [to Ashur] did battle.
29. [Wit]h the power of the great gods, my [lord]s
30. [aga]inst them I foug[ht].
31. [2]7,280 people, together with [their] chariots,
32. and the gods in whom they trusted, as spoil
33. I counted. Two-hundred chariots for [my] royal force
34. I collected from their midst.
35. The rest of them
36. I settled in the midst of Assyria
37. I repopulated Samerina more than before.
38. People from countries, conquered by my hands

39. I brought in it. My commissioner
40. I appointed as governor over
41. I counted them as Assyrians
    (Sargon II Nimrud Prism = RINAP II,074: IV: 25-41;
    Cogan 2021: 29).

The claims made in this text can only partly be corroborated by the archaeological and written evidence. Traces of the Israelite exile are clearly found in Assyrian inscriptions indicating that the exiled functioned in the agricultural scheme as well as in the military machine (see, e.g., Becking 1992: 61-93; Fales 2010: 117-40; Radner 2018). A few indications for the settlement of 'people from countries conquered by my (Sargon's) hand' have been excavated (see Becking 1992: 95-118; Faust 2021: 186-91). It is noteworthy that Sargon II does not claim the devastation of the city of Samaria in this inscription.[3] This 'silence' might be part of a Neo-Assyrian diplomatic ideology of not mentioning: it is also partly confirmed by the archaeological data and their interpretation. I here follow the convincing view of Forsberg (1995) and Tappy (2001), who challenged the traditional view based on Kenyon (1971) that all traces of demolition at Samaria should be connected to the Assyrian conquest. It seems better to accept that Sargon's army devastated only parts of the former capital. The line 'I repopulated Samerina more than before' cannot be substantiated by the demographic figures. The city of Samaria was never restored to its former glory (Aster 2019; see however the challenging remarks by Cogan 2022: 177-79). The only city the Neo-Assyrians restored was Megiddo, which functioned as a peripheral administrative center (Faust 2021: 139-80). It is noteworthy that after the Assyrian conquest, the production of olive oil in the territory of the Kingdom of Israel came to a halt. Archaeological evidence hints at a surplus production of olive oil in the eighth century but also to the demolition and non-restoration of the oil-presses by the Assyrians (see Wright and Elliott 2017: 444-48; Faust 2021: 53-59, 75-82, 134-38).

In sum: the archaeological evidence makes clear that the claims in the Inscription of Sargon are hyperbolic; they refer to ideology and not so much to facts on the ground. Next to that this inscription cannot be used as evidence for the *pax assyriaca* thesis.

---

3. This element is also absent in other inscriptions of Sargon II dealing with the conquest of Samaria, see Becking 1992: 25-33. It is only in Sargon II Display inscription from palace room XIV:15—which is of little historical significance—that Sargon is presented as the king who is made to declare: *aš-lul*, 'I plundered', Samaria (Becking 1992: 27-28).

3. With regard to the crown-witness for the prosperity that would have been the result of the *pax assyriaca*, the olive-oil industry at Ekron, Faust makes a set of noticeable remarks. First of all, he notes that Ekron—prospering in the seventh century—was neither a part of the province of Samerina nor of the client kingdom of Judah. The city was located in Philistine territory and part of a vassal state (Faust 2008: 182; 2021: 40). Secondly, he convincingly argues that the olive-oil production at Ekron was part of a greater economic scheme. The archaeological evidence hints at an agricultural pattern with the harbor city of Ashkelon at its center. In still wider circles there are areas with a dominant crop, although the soil could have been used for other cultivations. The first circle consists of the Philistine plain, with viniculture as its main vegetation. The second circle can be seen in the Shephalah hillside, producing mainly olive oil. A third circle is formed by the Judaean mountainous area, with a production of cereals. Finally, a fourth circle is the transitional space to the desert, with herding as its main activity. Since these cultivations are not directly prescribed by the conditions of the soil, Faust assumes an organizational scheme behind the division. He construes these facts as evidence of an economy in which agricultural products were taken to the harbor of Ashkelon—or made this movement possible by feeding the hinterland. Ashkelon was a pawn in the Phoenician trade around the Mediterranean. In sum, the produce was not intended for the Assyrian market but induced by the blossoming Phoenician economic power. This point is reinforced by the fact that in temple 650 at Ekron—a mid-seventh-century building—cultic influence from the Phoenician as well as from the Judaean realm is visible (Gitin 2012). Faust refers to the fact that in the lists of tribute paid to the Assyrians by the southwestern client kingdoms, only luxury items are mentioned and never agricultural products. The blossoming of the agricultural scheme just described made the supply of the luxury items by the vassals from Philistia and Judah possible. By implication, the Ekron olive oil industry cannot be interpreted as a result of the *pax assyriaca* (Faust and Weiss 2005; Faust 2011; 2021: 116-38; Faust and Weiss 2011; Maeir, Welch and Eniukhina 2021).

4. The *pax assyriaca* thesis presupposes a clear presence of Neo-Assyrian administration in the newly established provinces in the Levant. In the provinces closer to the Assyrian core land, three kinds of footsteps of the Assyrian administration are found: (1) administrative texts, (2) palaces and comparable buildings, and (3) Assyrian Palace Ware. In his assessment of the *pax assyriaca* thesis, Faust is looking for these footsteps in the province of Samerina (Faust 2021: 139-80).

Administrative texts. In a Neo-Assyrian letter, King Sargon II expresses his preference for the use of Akkadian—although Aramaic is permitted—

in administrative and diplomatic texts: 'Why would you not write and send me messages in Akkadian?':

> [As to what you wrote]: 'There are informers [... to the king] and coming to his presence; if it is acceptable to the king, let me write and send my messages to the king on Aram[aic] parchment sheets' — why would you not write and send me messages in Akkadian (*ak-ka-da-at-tu*)? Really, the message which you write in it must be drawn up in this very manner — this is a fixed regulation!
> (Letter to Sin-iddina CT 54 101 = SAA 17.2: 18-19; see Fales 2010: 63-64; Aster and Faust 2015: 295; Faust 2021: 139, 144-45; the letter on crimes—SAA 16.63—refers to messages both in Assyrian and in Aramaic)

This implies that cuneiform texts are more than indicative for the presence of Assyrian administration. The number of cuneiform texts from the seventh century BCE excavated in the territory of the province Samerina is surprisingly low. At Samaria—the official capital of the province—one administrative text, an inscription on a bulla with the Assyrian royal seal, an inscribed cylinder seal and one royal inscription were found (Becking 1992: 112-14; Horowitz and Oshima 2006: 113-15; Faust 2021: 139-45). The administrative text contains a court order commissioning the settler ᵖ*A-a* PAP.MEŠ (Aja-Ache) to pay the city governor six oxen and over twelve sheep, probably as his part of the tribute to Assyria. The inscription on the bulla indicates that someone in Samaria had received a royal letter. The cylinder seal is a luxury object not made for real use since its inscription is in positive, which would result in inverted cuneiform in an impression. The royal inscription is too fragmentary to read. Together they indicate the—expected—presence of Assyrian administration in a provincial capital (Faust 2021: 141). Other cuneiform texts from this period were mainly found in a relative small area.[4] In Gezer, two administrative texts were found (Becking 1992: 114-18; Horowitz and Oshima 2006: 55-59; Aster and Faust 2015; Na'aman 2016: 276-77; Faust 2021: 141), indicating that Assyrian rules and conventions regarding the sale of plots of lands were in use. The same must be said about the two Neo-Assyrian inscriptions found at nearby Tel-Hadidi (edited by Na'aman and Zadok 2000; see Aster and Faust 2015; Faust 2021: 141; Na'aman 2016: 27). They indicate that among the deported settlers in Tel Hadidi, the same Assyrian rules were adopted. At the site of Ben Shemen—not far away from Gezer and Tel Hadidi—a

---

4. Two other cuneiform inscriptions were found, but more to the north: (1) a fragment of a royal stele at Qaqun still to be published, but probably a fragment from the stele found at Ben Shemen (see Cogan 2008); and (2) a hardly legible inscription from Kh. Kusiya (Horowitz and Oshima 2006: 100-101).

Neo-Assyrian royal inscription was excavated. Only seven lines were preserved. They read:

1.] x
2. KU]R *Mu*-[*ṣur*   I uprooted from Egypt ...
3.] MUḪ (?)   over Egypt ...
4.] LÚ.N[AM.MEŠ   kings, governors ...
5. *eš-šú-*]-*ti*   I reappointed ...
6. AN.]ŠAR *u* DI[NGIR.MEŠ   Ashur and the great gods
7. *dà*]-*ri*-[*šam*   I set for all times ...

(Sargon II Ben Shemen stela; see Cogan 2008; supplemented on the basis of the comparable phraseology in Esarhaddon Zendjirli Stele = Borger 1956 § 65)

These five finds were made in a limited region in the southwestern tip of the province of Samerina that might have functioned as a guard post to the adjacent client kingdoms in Philistia and Judah (Aster and Faust 2015; Faust 2021: 141-45). With Faust, I arrive at the conclusion that the evidence from the written texts for a supposed Assyrian administrative grip on the province is too meagre.

Palaces and comparable buildings. If the Assyrians had been actively organizing a scheme bringing prosperity and welfare to the southwestern Levant, they would have needed administrative buildings to coordinate their operations. Archaeological traces have been found of Assyrian building activities in and around the province of Samerina (see Faust 2021: 153-59). Remains of palaces and administrative buildings, however, have not been unearthed. The only two possible remnants of such buildings could be the complex 1052/1369 from Megiddo (Kertai 2018: 150) and Building T1-3/1 from the Neo-Assyrian stratum at Tel Dan (Thereani 2019: 221). The lack of small finds that could illuminate the function of the building at Megiddo in the newly built provincial capital make a classification as administrative building, however, unlikely (Faust 2021: 159). At Tel Dan various types of pottery were found connected to Building T1-3/1 (Thereani 2109: 221-23). The character of these finds is too unspecific to make a connection with the presence of Assyrian administration. The only clear sign of Assyrian control was excavated at Tel Hadidi. The complex in which the two inscriptions mentioned above were found can be interpreted as a *Bīt Mardīti*, 'road station'. This station would have been part of the network of Neo-Assyrian roads throughout the empire. These roads were used for trade transport and postal services. At a *Bīt Mardīti*, the horses could be refreshed (Aster 2015; Na'aman 2019). The presence of this station should be construed as an instrument by which the Assyrians controlled the flow of trade. Remains of an Iron Age Assyrian fortress were excavated at Tell Qudadi along the Mediterranean coast. This fort would indicate that the Assyrians reinforced their control of the trade route along the *Via Maris* (Fantalkin and Tal 2009).

Assyrian Palace Ware. In the Neo-Assyrian Empire a group of luxury ceramics have been found, labelled by modern scholars as Assyrian Palace Ware (Oates 1959; Hunt 2015; Faust 2021: 160-62). These exquisitely made items were produced in limited numbers and served the elite at their banquets. Owning and displaying such vessels were symbols of power and membership in the highest classes at and around the court. Examples of this ware have been found in the Assyrian core area but also in some provinces, especially in Dur-Katlimmu and Guzanu. The presence of this ware hints at an Assyrian influence on the social structure of the provinces (Hunt 2015: 97-145). In case the *pax assyriaca* thesis were correct, Assyrian Palace Ware should have reached the elite in the province of Samerina—circles around the governor and befriended local leaders. The problem, however, is that less than a handful of locally produced imitations have been found (Faust 2021: 162-63). The only real Assyrian Palace Ware found in the southern Levant were unearthed at Tel Keisan, Tell el-Hesi and Tel Jemmeh, all three within the borders of a client kingdom (Engstrom 2004; Hunt 2015: 146-81; Zilberg 2015; Faust 2021: 163-66). This presence can be connected to the fact that the vassal kingdoms were of greater importance to the Assyrians in view of their ability to provide tribute. This absence of real Assyrian Palace Ware is paralleled by the scarcity of other objects that could have referred to a Neo-Assyrian administrative grip, such as glazed pottery, Assyrian seals, weights and measures. The few items, however, were locally produced (see Faust 2021: 166-71).

2.2.3. Conclusion

All in all, although the *pax assyriaca* thesis might be illustrative for the situation in other parts of the Neo-Assyrian Empire, it does not fit the province of Samerina. During the Neo-Assyrian times this area was an unimportant and impoverished backwater. This conclusion also implies that the thesis cannot be used in a discourse negating the reality of trauma.

2.3. Assyrian Religion in Judah and Samerina

2.3.1. The Assumption

In their annals, the Assyrian kings claim that their victories in the expansion phase of the empire are a result of their faith and trust in the 'great gods of Assyria'. This claim implies weakness on the side of the deities of the conquered nations. In the vassal treaties and loyalty oath, the vassal kings are invited to make their vows in front of the same 'great gods of Assyria':

> (concerning Assurbanipal, the great crown prince designate, son of Esarhaddon, king of Assyria, on behalf of whom he has concluded this treaty with you)
> which he) confirmed, made and concluded in the presence of Jupiter, Venus, Saturn, Mercury, Mars and Sirius;
> in the presence of Aššur, Anu, Ill[il], Ea, Sin, Šamaš, Adad, Marduk, Nabû, Nusku, Uraš, Nergal, Mullissu, Šerua, Belet-ili, Ištar of Nineveh, Ištar of Arbela, the gods dwelling in heaven and earth, the gods of Assyria, the gods of Sumer and [Akka]d, all the gods of the lands.
> Sw[ear ea]ch individually by Aššur, father of the gods, lord of the lands!
> Ditto by Anu, Illil and Ea!
> Ditto by Sin, Šamaš, Adad and Marduk!
> Ditto by Nabû, Nusku, Uraš and Nergal!
> Ditto by Mullissu, Šerua and Belet-ili!
> Ditto by Ištar of Nineveh and Ištar of Arbela!
> Ditto by all the gods of the Inner City!
> Ditto by all the gods of Nineveh!
> Ditto by all the gods of Calah!
> Ditto by all the gods of Arbela!
> Ditto by all the gods of Kilizi!
> Ditto by all the gods of Harran!
> Ditto by all the gods of Babylon, Borsippa and Nippur!
> Ditto by all the gods of Assyria!
> Ditto by all the gods of Sumer and Akkad!
> Ditto by all the gods of the lands; ditto by all the gods of heaven and earth! Ditto by all the gods of one's land and one's district!
> (Esarhaddon Succession Treaty SAA 2.6: 11-40; see Cogan 2021: 132-42, 188-92)

These remarks have led to the assumption that the Assyrians would have imposed the veneration of their main gods on the conquered territories at the dispense of local cults (first by Olmstaed 1931: 452-85; see also Jeremias 1970: 24; Spieckermann 1982: 307-72).

This assumption of oriental religious imperialism, however, for the continuity of local cults throughout the empire, including Israel and Judah, has been challenged on the basis of written texts and archaeological evidence (McKay 1973; Cogan 1974, 1993, 2021; Matarese 2021: 214-17). These scholars proposed that it would be better to construe that the Assyrian religion was imposed only on the vassal king and his court and might have been restricted to the moments of diplomatic encounter (McKay 1973; Cogan 1974; see also Berlejung 2012: 21-59; Cogan 2021).

2.3.2. The Evidence

I will discuss a set of elements that are related to the question whether or not the conquered areas and the client kingdoms had to adopt the Assyrian religion.

The altar from Damascus. In the book of Kings, it is narrated that Ahaz of Judah—after his submission as a vassal to Tiglath Pileser III—visited this king in Damascus. During this visit he saw an altar, a copy of which he had built for the temple of YHWH in Jerusalem, replacing the bronze altar made by Solomon. The former altar was moved to a different spot and henceforth functioned for royal divination (2 Kgs 16.10-16).

Traditionally, the erection of this new altar has been interpreted as summoned by the Assyrian king and construed as a means to install the cult of Ashur in Jerusalem (Olmstead 1931: 452; Soggin 1985: 228). This view is, however, problematic. The text in 2 Kings does not label the altar as Assyrian; it just mentions its existence. The text in 2 Kings lays the initiative to build the altar in the hands of Ahaz. Within the text he is not forced by the Assyrian king. In the reports on the reforms by Hezekiah (2 Kgs 18:4) and Josiah (2 Kgs 23:11-14) the altar of Ahaz is not mentioned and hence not seen as idolatrous or foreign. To John McKay and Morton Cogan, these observations form evidence not to construe the altar from Damascus as an element of Assyrian enforcement (McKay 1973: 5-12; Cogan 1974: 73-77; see also Nelson 1986; Cogan 1993; Berlejung 2012; Cogan 2021: 51-53; unconvincing criticism in Spieckermann 1982: 374-75). In their opinion, the altar was erected as part of a broader programme to bring the cult of YHWH up to date. Nili Wazana even supposes that the altar was part of a Yahwistic cult at Damascus (Wazana 2016). Natalie May, correctly, argued that the erection of this altar by Ahaz was a token of his wish to imitate his superiors (May 2022a: 178-82).

2 Kings 16 narrates still another building activity by Ahaz that needs to be taken into consideration:

> And the covered way for the Sabbath that had been built inside the house and the outer entrance for the king he [=Ahaz] caused to go around the house of the Lord, because of the king of Assyria. (2 Kgs 16.18 ESV).[5]

---

5. The translation of the final three Hebrew words is disputed. Some render '... before the face of the king of Assyria', i.e. so that he could not see the architectural elements. The compound *mippānîm* indicates, however, the reason for an action.

Whatever the exact character of this reconstruction, the text is clear that it was made 'because of the king of Assyria'. This adverbial adjunct can be construed as connected to the acts in v. 18 alone, but also to the whole of 10-18. In sum: at least some accommodations were made to please the king of Assyria. The cult as such, however, remained Yahwistic.

Astralization of the Divine. Thanks to the work of the Othmar Keel and his students, we now have a better insight in the way the divine was depicted in ancient Israel and especially in the changes of repertoire over the ages. It turns out that in the Assyrian period the traditional images of God faded away. The representation of the divine as a strong animal, a lion for instance, or as the ruling sun, made way for the use of astral bodies such as the moon and the stars (Keel and Uehlinger 1992: 322-59). It would be, however, a mistake to construe the Assyrian influence as the only force behind this change. As Keel and Uehlinger (1992) have made clear, other influences such as the Aramaic, the Phoenician, and the Egyptian too were instrumental. It would therefore be more correct to interpret this shift as an indication of the globalization of the religious culture of—most probably the elite of—ancient Israel.

I will discuss only a few items in this connection. Excavations at Dothan revealed a cylinder seal most probably from the end of the eighth century (edited by Keel 1977: 95, Fig. 221; see Keel and Uehlinger 1992: 327-30, Fig. 281). This seal depicts a scene in which an Assyrian official brings an offering on an altar. The symbols in the upper part of the scene, a crescent and an octagonal star, make clear that the official is presented as loyal to the moon god Sin. The seal probably belonged to an Assyrian official who reciprocally would show his loyalty to the Assyrian king. Other cylinder seals show the veneration of other Mesopotamian and Aramaic deities (Keel and Uehlinger 1992: 331-35). It should be noted that these few seals are to be connected to the Assyrian administration in Judah and their Judahite companions and hence do not reveal the religious ideas of greater parts of the population (Faust 2021: 167).

Astral symbols quite often appear on seals from Iron Age IIC, the Assyrian period. They have been found throughout Judah and can sociologically be connected to the local, that is, indigenous administration. This becomes clear from the fact that some seals are inscribed with the names of their owners, who have clear Jahwistic names (Keel and Uehlinger 1992: 340-61). An interesting example can be found on a sale contract from Gezer dated to the middle of the seventh century (Becking 1982/83; Keel and Uehlinger 1992: 340-41). The inscription administers the sale of a plot of land by *na-tan-ia-u*, 'Nethanya', a Judaean or an Israelite. The names of the witnesses can be construed as Egyptian, Aramaic and Akkadian, all indicating a mixed population in Gezer in Assyrian times. The cuneiform tablet contains a seal impression that I connect to Netanyahu. The seal depicts the lunar symbol of the moon god Sin and a hexagonal star above a table or an altar. This seal makes clear that the astral-image language was present also at the fringes of Judah.

Of great importance in this connection is a group of half a dozen scaraboids. The engraved picture on them presents a deity sitting on a throne, which is in most cases placed on a bark. Above the deity, astral symbols are engraved: the moon and a star. In front of the deity, an *anch*-symbol is placed (Keel and Uehlinger 1992: 349-56). According to Keel and Uehlinger, the enthroned deity is a representation of '*ēl*, 'El', and could refer to the God of Judah.

The astralization of the divine is evident. It cannot be construed as imposed on Judah and Israel by the Assyrian military and administrative presence. It is more correct to interpret this change of a broader acculturation to Aramaic and Assyrian habits or the trend of the time (Cooley 2011). Since the iconographic material only gives insight into the upper layers of the local communities, no conclusions can be drawn as to the character of the religious views at the level of tribe or family.

Mesopotamian deities in Judah and Israel. There is only sparse evidence for the veneration of Assyrian deities in the province of Samerina or in the vassal kingdom of Judah. Excavations in the Shephelah brought to light the fragment of a Lamashtu plaque (Cogan 1995). This plaque was most probably an apotropaic amulet used in defense against the evil forces of this demon (Zilberg 2016: 385). Excavations at Tell Miqne-Ekron brought to light a silver pendant from the seventh century BCE depicting the goddess Ištar standing on a lion (Golani and Sass 1998: 71, Fig. 14:2; Moriconi and Tucci 2015: 500). This precious object was probably owned by a rich person and is not to be seen as evidence for the cult of Ishtar in the vassal kingdom of Judah since it was found in Philistine Ekron. Excavations at Gezer brought to light a locally made Neo-Assyrian cylinder seal depicting a hunting god—probably Ninurta—riding on a hybrid animal, a lion-griffin (Ornan, Ortiz and Wolff 2013). It is uncertain whether this seal was owned by a person from the Assyrian occupation or by an Assyrian-minded local.

Strange customs are referred to by Zephaniah. In the prophetic books from the Hebrew Bible, the Israelites and Judahites are constantly and vehemently rebuked for their moral and religious trespasses. Quite often, this prophetic criticism is formulated in vague language and standard phrases, such as 'they went after other gods' or 'they did what is wrong in the eyes of YHWH'. It should be noted that in the original communication this language was construed as less vague, since the audience would have understood its meaning. Occasionally, the reproaches are more precise and concrete. I will consider a few examples from the book of Zephaniah. There exists an abundant literature on the date of the original composition of that book and its—to some scholars complex—redaction history. For now, it suffices to accept that the prophetic activity of Zephaniah took place in the final decades of the Assyrian Empire, which is about a dozen years before the reformation of Josiah.

In a prophecy of doom, Zephaniah reproaches the inhabitants of the city of Jerusalem. He announces that YHWH will cut them off from that place:

> those who prostrate themselves on the rooftops
>   to the host of heaven
> and those who prostrate themselves
>   […] Milcom (Zeph. 1.5)[6]

Zephaniah is criticizing the syncretistic religion in Jerusalem. He condemns people who venerate deities other than YHWH. Two of them are named. The 'bowing down to the host of heaven' refers clearly to the veneration of astral bodies (see also Jer. 19.13). In traditional Yahwism, YHWH was seen as a warrior god surrounded by a heavenly army (see, e.g., Josh. 5.13-15). In the last century of the monarchic period the connotation of the words 'the host of heaven' has changed into an indication of 'astral deities', comparable to the gods whose symbols were depicted on the seals and scaraboids mentioned above. They cannot be construed as part of a cult that was imposed on Judah by the Assyrians. Their veneration is a sign of the adaptation by the elite in Jerusalem to the general Assyro-Aramaic cultural tendencies in the seventh century (Sweeney 2003: 70-71; Cooley 2011).

Milcom was the head of the Ammonite pantheon. The scarce pieces of evidence on the Transjordanian deity make clear that his veneration would not have differed much from the veneration of YHWH in Judah and Israel. Tradition has it that Solomon introduced the cult of Milcom in Jerusalem to please some of his wives (1 Kgs 11.5, 33). The reform of Josiah (see below) tried to end his veneration. The mention of Milcom in Zeph. 1.5 cannot be construed as an indication of any form of religious politics by the Assyrians. The text is evidence for the syncretistic cult in Jerusalem in the seventh century (Sweeney 2003: 70-71; Levin 2012; Dietrich 2016: 204-205).

---

6. The final word of the verse, *mlkm*, has been rendered by various ancient versions as referring to the Ammonite deity Milcom. The rereading of the word as *malkām*, 'their king', by the Masoretes provoked the inclusion of a gloss ('to the sun, moon, and stars. They swear by YHWH, and swear by') in which 'their king' is connected to YHWH. For details see, e.g., Berlin 1994: 75-76; Sweeney 2003: 55-72; Dietrich 2016: 204-205; Cogan 2021: 147.

A few verses later Zephaniah announces divine judgment:

> I shall punish the officials and the king's sons,
>   and all who clothe themselves in foreign attire. (Zeph. 1.8)

In this reproach there is more at stake than prophetic dislike of fashion trends. The Hebrew noun *malbûš*, 'garment, attire', denotes various kinds of official and cultic garments expressing the higher social status of the person dressed with it. Dressing in foreign attire of leading persons in Jerusalem is rebuked by the prophet as a means of breaking the code and accepting the foreign as more important than the local (Uehlinger 1996; Sweeney 2003: 85). Again, it cannot be decided whether this trend was imposed by the Assyrians or just another form of local adaptation of the international trend. Natalie May referred to an analogy from Zinjirli (Sam'al). On a Phoenician stele of King Kalamuwa, the Anatolian king is depicted as if he were an Assyrian ruler wearing the attire of an Assyrian king (*KAI* 24). It is uncertain whether he presented himself this way in imitation of his Assyrian superiors or that he was forced to do so (May 2022a: 171-75).

Zephaniah 1.9 contains the at first sight enigmatic words:

> And I will punish on that day all who leap over the threshold,
>   who fill the house of their lord with violence and deceit.

The conceptual coherence between the two lines in this verse can be cleared by assuming that 'leaping over the threshold' is an act of entering the temple by by-passing the guardian snake-like demons that were protecting the entrance to the sanctuary. Zephaniah refers to a traditional element in folk religion in which snakes were seen as gatekeepers for divine realms. This tradition is already attested in the proto-Phoenician parts of the serpent spells in third millennium Egyptian pyramid texts, in a second millennium Hittite instruction to priests and temple officials, and in a first millennium description of Philistine religious customs.[7] The presence of this traditional view on liminal space is hence to be seen as the revival of indigenous folk religion and cannot be connected to Assyrian influence (Becking 2014; Dietrich 2016: 209).

The assumption that Zephaniah is especially rebuking the leading circles in Jerusalem for their religious and moral behaviour can be reinforced by the observation that in Zeph. 2.1-3 he is presenting the lower classes as persons of good conduct (Dietrich 2016: 210-11).

Royal ideology: Ashurbanipal and Psalm 72. In 668 Ashurbanipal (*Aššur-bāni-apli*) accessed the throne of Assyria. He would become the

---

7. PT 232-238; 281-282; 286-287; see Steiner 2011; KUB 13.4 = *CTH* 264 iii 55-83; 1 Sam. 5.5.

last great ruler of the Neo-Assyrian Empire. The decline—already visible during his reign—continued after his death in 627. His successors were unable to turn the tide and to stop the Neo-Babylonian conquests. On the occasion of his coronation during the New Year festival, a hymn was composed that gave words of high hopes for the reign of the new king (SAA 3.11). The hymn contains the language and the worldview of the traditional Mesopotamian royal ideology. The great gods of Assyria are invoked to support the new king and bless his reign:

> May Šamaš, king of heaven and earth, elevate you to shepherdship over the four [region]s!
> May Aššur, who ga[ve y]ou [the sceptre], lengthen your days and years!
> Spread your land wide at your feet!
> May Šerua extol [your name] to your god! (SAA 3.11:1-4)

The kingship will be based on the divine rule of Ashur:

> Aššur is king — indeed Aššur is king!
> Assurbanipal is the [representative] of Aššur, the creation of his hands. (SAA 3.11:15; Fales 2010: 80-81)

The blessing by the gods will become visible in three features: the duration of his reign, the economic flowering of Assyria during his kingship, and the presence of *ket-ti me-šá-ru*, 'truth (and) justice', in his command. The wish for the endurance of his reign is phrased eloquently:

> Give our lord Assurbanipal long [days], copious years, strong [wea]pons, a long reign, y[ear]s of abundance, a good name, [fame], happiness and joy, auspicious oracles, and leadership over (all other) kings. (SAA 3.11:r.1)

The well-being of the nation is phrased in purely economic terms, applying low market prices as a sign of prosperity:

> May [the people] of Assur buy 30 kor of grain for one shekel of silver!
> May [the peopl]e of Assur buy 3 seah of oil for one shekel of silver!
> May [the peop]le of Assur buy 30 minas of wool for one shekel of silver! (SAA 3.11:9)

The theme of justice is slightly underdeveloped in the hymn except for the gift of *ket-ti me-šá-ru*, 'truth (and) justice', and the metaphor of the shepherd.

Martin Arneth has convincingly argued that Psalm 72 was composed on the model of the Assyrian hymn for the coronation of the Judaean king Josiah. His comparison of the two texts yields some interesting points. Both texts reflect the ancient Near Eastern royal ideology, be it with different nuances. In both texts, the earthly king is construed as the representative of the solar deity. Both texts contain a *speculum regale* with moral summons. Important differences can be found in the fact that the royal rule in Psalm 72 has no universal dimensions as in the coronation hymn as well in the fact that in Psalm 72 the royal justice is connected to the theme of care for the *personae miserae*. Although the texts are composed in two different languages, words and phrases in Psalm 72 reveal knowledge of the Assyrian counterpart. The Psalm is clearly composed after the Assyrian model. Since Psalm 72 is apparently addressed to a young king, the enthronement of the eight-year-old Josiah seems to be a logical context for the composition of the Hebrew text.

In applying the concept of the Assyrian example, circles around the court adapted the Mesopotamian view on kingship. Nevertheless, the differences between both texts indicate that the Psalm was written in a period in which the striving for independence in Judah slowly awoke.

Continuing syncretistic Yahwism. The Hebrew Bible seems to present a monotheistic form of religion. Various texts refer to the veneration of only one God. One can think of the oneness-creed in Deut. 6.4 or of texts in the second part in the book called Isaiah. In these splendid chapters from Isaiah 40 onward, Yhwh is praised as the only deity worth the reverence of the Israelites. The 'other gods' are set aside as manufactured by humankind. The earth in its entirety is summoned to venerate this deity. This belief system can be classified as exclusive monotheism, since the veneration of this one deity is presented as the only possibility for all human beings. Other deities might have been venerated by some persons; they are seen, however, as powerless entities.

However, there are many textual and archaeological signs that the religion in ancient Israel has not always been monotheistic or monolatrous through the ages. The fact that prophets continuously warn against the cult(s) of 'other deities' can only be read as a signal that these deities were venerated by many Israelites and Judaeans. Archaeology has revealed three important groups of evidence for polytheism in ancient Israel.

The first group is formed by the various standing stones throughout Israel/Canaan in the Middle and Late Bronze periods onward, continuing into the late Iron Age (see Mettinger 1995). These stones, referred to as *maṣṣēbôt* in the Hebrew Bible, quite often are found in sets of three or five, mainly in a cultic context close to the city gates. These standing stones represent local deities and deified ancestors. They functioned in the cult of the ancestors as well as divine guarantors for the judicial processes in 'the gate' that were instrumental for the continuation of city and clan.

The second group is formed by the so-called 'pillar-figurines'. About a thousand of them have been found from all eras of ancient Israel, including the Assyrian period. These figurines represent a nude goddess with explicit breasts. These figurines should be construed as an indication of the fact that in the religious symbol system at the family level a deity Asherah played an important role. At this level she is a protecting *dea nutrix* who could be evoked in times of danger and despair, especially in the process of giving birth. The breasts so manifestly present in many pillar figurines should not be construed as an erotic symbol, but as referring to the heavenly milk that Mother Earth is giving to the poor and the needy. Ian Wilson has argued that the figurines represent one attempt to maintain local identity as the Neo-Assyrian Empire rapidly expanded and absorbed much of the region (Wilson 2012). He is correct in seeing them as a sign of the continuation of local polytheistic lore, but I doubt that the figurines had an anti-Assyrian impact.

Thirdly, at Khirbet al-Qom a palaeo-Hebrew inscription was found in a tomb dating from the late eighth century. The text is incised on a stone above the image of a blessing(?) hand and reads:

> Uriyahu the honourable has written this
> Blessed be Uriyahu by Yahweh
> And [because?] from his oppressors by his Asherah he has saved him
> [written] by Oniyahu
> ... by his Asherah
> ... and his Asherah. (Renz 1995: 47-64, 202-11)

This inscription makes clear that the veneration of Asherah as consort of God, already evidenced by the inscription from Kuntillet Ajrud, continued into the Assyrian period.

Textual signs are of course difficult to date and hence uncertain to argue with as witnesses for the religion in Judah during the Assyrian period. Some Psalms, however, relate to a symbol system in which more than one god is venerated. Psalms 58 and 82 contain the concept that YHWH stands among or above the other deities. Here YHWH is part of a heavenly council. Of special interest is Psalm 91. This hymn on trust among the dangers and threats of life mentions YHWH:

> He will cover you with his wings
>   You will be safe in his care
> His faithfulness will protect
>   And defend you.

But in vv. 5 and 6 we read:

> You need not fear for the terror of the night
>   For the arrow that flies at daytime
> For the pestilence that goes around in the dark
>   Or the demon that destroys at midday.

These four nouns—'terror of the night', 'arrow', 'pestilence' and 'midday demon'—refer to threatening demons that were seen as part of daily life (Vreugdenhil 2020).

The textual and archaeological evidence together strongly suggests the continuation of a form of Yahwism that would vary from city to village and that incorporated the veneration of deities other than Yahweh.

2.3.2. Conclusion on Religion

Religion in Judah in the Assyrian era was a multifaceted feature. As a vassal, the king had to adhere to the Mesopotamian deities. The Assyrians, however, did not force the Judaeans to their religion. The elite in Jerusalem had an inclination to be part of a more international and cosmopolitical culture. The majority of the population continued their locally different forms of Yahwism. Unease with the economic and religious liberalism of Manasseh led to orthodox forms of Yahwism (Cogan 2021).

2.4. In Sum: Between Byron and *Pax Assyriaca*

These considerations lead to the conclusion that the Assyrian grip on the southwestern provinces and vassal kingdoms can neither be construed as a politico-economical construction that led to greater welfare and prosperity all over nor to a forced conversion to the religion of the conquerors. A nuanced view of the reality is needed that will be outlined in the next chapter. In other words, both Byron's dark words, 'The Assyrian came down like the wolf on the fold', and the optimistic view of an Assyrian peace miss the complexity of the reality in that age (Byron 1903: 222).

3

Trauma Experienced (the 'Reality')

3.1 What Really Happened—a Methodological Warning

It would be nice if we were able to (re)construct what happened under the yoke of Assur. This historical exercise is, however, complicated for several reasons (see the essays in Becking 2021).

1. So-called sources—both written and pictorial—are complex entities. They contain a set of individual propositions on the past or claims for the existence of events, but are glued together in a narrative or visual design.
2. The narrative structure as a whole—or the pictorial design as such—is the intermediary that is created by the narrator, or historian, to convince the readership of the truth of his or her view of the events. It is for this reason that a historian has to deconstruct a given source in search of trustworthy particles. Only then can a text, the Hebrew Bible or an Assyrian inscription, be seen as a 'source of information' at the level of its various particles, but not at the level of the text as a whole (see also Frahm 2019).
3. Collingwood tried to overcome the dilemma between 'realism' and 'scepticism' by elaborating a view on the character of so-called historical sources. These traces of the past are available and knowable in the present. All the historian has in hand are the particles of evidence mirroring the past. The evidence makes it possible to know the past but only in a restricted way. The task of the historian is to collect as much evidence as possible and then construct a personal image of the past. In this re-enactment, models and imagination play a role. The historian cannot do without metaphorical language to describe in an approximating and incomplete way the events mirrored in the sources (see Collingwood 1994).
4. Texts are therefore not neutral containers. The narrator made the selection out of the available material and connected this selection into the order of the given text or image. The reader is thus forced to look at

the basic narration that became text in a narrative, the way the narrator wants the reader to look at it. The narrator is like the hole in a shoebox through which the diorama can be seen. The narrator of a text is hence in a power position, and the reader is dependent on this peephole. It is the narrator who forces me to look at the ensemble of the narrative as it is arranged by the narrator and especially from his or her point of view. There are no neutral reports.

5. The relative scarcity of the traces of past human behaviour in the Assyrian century makes it difficult to weigh the evidence. Is the piece found representative of the past or does it represent a fortuitous minority case? Is, for instance, the finding of one piece of Assyrian Palace Ware at one tell telling us that at every tell such ware can be found or is it just a single haphazard piece?

These warnings do not imply that it is completely impossible to write a history of Judah and Israel during the Assyrian age. They only hint at the fact that the text below is my construction of this part of the past and that it is open for debate (see further Lorentz 1997). Finally, it should be noted that in case the historical reality could be represented, the question how people experienced the events is unanswerable in view of the scarcity—or the almost non-existence—of ego documents in which victims reflected the assumedly traumatic disruption of their lives.

3.2 Elements of Disruption

3.2.1 The Shadow Sides of the Assyrian Warfare

The Assyrians boasted of their military victories both in the inscriptions and in the palace reliefs. They present their war efforts as being instrumental to the will of the gods concerning those nations who trespassed. Many examples could have been given; I chose the description of the campaign of Sargon II against Kiakki of [the ci]ty Šinuḫtu as described on a wall slab from Room XIV of his palace at Khorsabad:

> In my fourth regnal year, Kiakki of [the ci]ty Šinuḫtu disregarded the treaty (sworn) by the great gods and [be]came dilatory about delivering (his) tribute. I raised my hand(s) to the gods, my lords, overwhelmed his royal city Šinuḫtu like a [f]og, and counted him as booty, together with his fighting men, his wife, his sons, his daughters, [(his) pro]perty (and) possessions, the treasure of his palace, (along) with 7,350 people of his land. I gave his royal city Šinuḫtu

to Kurtî of the land Atuna; I made larger than before (the number/ amount of) [ho]rses, mules, gold, (and) silver (that he had to pay as tribute) and I imposed (this) upon him
(Sargon II Khorsabad Room XIV, RINAP 2, 004: 6'-12').

In this same inscription, the dark side of the Assyrian warfare is shown:

[Then, o]n Mount Uauš, the mountain [wh]ere they had thrown down the corpse of Azâ, I flayed the skin from Bag-dāti [and] (then) showed (it) to the people of the land Man[ne]a.
(Sargon II Khorsabad Room XIV, RINAP 2, 004: 23'-26'; campaign against Ursa of Urartu // Sargon II Khorsabad Room II, RINAP 2, 001: 82-83)

In a display inscription from Khorsabad, it is narrated:

I captured [Ḫ]anūnu (Ḫanno) and brought him in bondage to my city Aššur; I then destroyed, demolished, (and) burned down with fire [the city Rap]ḫia. I carried off as booty 9,033 people together with their numerous possessions.
(Sargon II Khorsabad Room II, RINAP 2, 001: 55-56; campaign against Gaza).

In his report on the conquest of the rebellious city Damdammusa, Assurnasirpal II wrote:

I felled with the sword 800 of their combat troops, I burnt 3,000 captives from them. I did not leave one of them alive as hostage. I captured alive Hulaya their city ruler. I made a pile of their corpses. I burnt their adolescent boys (and) girls. I flayed Hulaya their city ruler (and) draped his skin over the wall of the city. . . .
(Grayson 1976: II 547-50; see Cogan 1983; Dubovský 2009; cf. 2 Kgs 15.16; the theme is adapted by Sargon II Annals from Khorsabad: 169 = *COS* 2.118A; Sargon II Display Inscription: 35)

In the inscriptions of Ashurnasirpal II, eight acts of the cruelty of burning enemies made captives are to be found. I will give one example from the report on the conquest of the city of Tela:

Many captives from them I burnt with fire [...] I burnt their boys (and) their girls as a burnt offering.
(Grayson 1991 A.0.101.1: i 116, ii 1; A.0.101.17: ii 1; Dewar 2021)

No mention of infanticide, however, is made in the inscriptions of the Sargonic kings. This might indicate a growing awareness of humanitarian feelings.

The walls in the palaces built by the Neo-Assyrian kings were decorated with reliefs. They depicted the glorious acts of the Assyrian army in battle.

These scenes from the battlefield had a double function. On the one hand they glorified the various kings and must have made a great impression on their subjects. On the other hand, these depictions were signs of warnings to the rulers of the client kingdoms or vassal states who came for an audience to the palace. The graphic scenes of Assyrian victory discouraged those vassals who were thinking about throwing off the Assyrian yoke.

These reliefs contain horrific details concerning the dark side of the Assyrian warfare. The sculpturers quite openly depicted the atrocities. I will give a few examples:

FIGURE 1: akg-images / Erich Lessing

- In the Lachish Reliefs, which depict the siege and conquest of the Assyrian king Sennacherib of the Judaean city of Lachish, a scene occurs in which two Assyrian soldiers erect a stake with an impaled, naked man, most probably already dead, beside two others (Ussishkin 1982; see FIGURE 1).
- After his campaign against the rebellious Elamites, Ashurbanipal had pictures made of the mass deportation of the Elamites (Walker 2022: 126-83). In one scene, two Elamites are depicted as fastened to the ground. Assyrian soldiers triumphantly walk around with the heads of the decapitated Elamites in their hands (Bonatz 2004).
- Relief BM 124927, now in the British Museum, quite exceptionally depicts the acts of Assyrian soldiers slaying pregnant Arab women on their road to deportation in the reign of Ashurbanipal (see Dubovský 2009).

Both lists, the textual as well as the pictorial, could easily be expanded with dozens of other examples of Assyrian war crimes. This indicates the yearly practice of the Neo-Assyrian army (Timmer 2020: 25-36). Written examples regarding the conquest of Samaria by Sargon II or the siege of Jerusalem by Sennacherib do not contain elements of this dehumanizing language. This absence, however, is not compelling evidence that the Assyrians would have treated Samaria and Judah in a more elegant way. The fragment from the Lachish Relief discussed above can be seen as an indication that the Assyrians did not change their habits for the occasion.

Memories of such atrocities or even the rumor of them could have installed trauma in the collective soul in Judah and in Israel.

3.2.2 *The Disbalance between Deportation and Resettlement*

Deportation is a perennial political means of disruption and disordering the resistance against a predominant power. It consists in a forced migration of great numbers of people to places 'where they did not wish to go' (see Gospel of John 21.18). Such a migration implied the refraction of communities and families as supportive networks and the end of a traditional lifestyle. The aim of these deportations was twofold. On the one hand, the Assyrians tried to break the resistance against their empire by scattering disobedient persons throughout the empire, and on the other hand, the deported persons were a welcome reinforcement of both the military and the agricultural ranks (Sano 2020). To feed the growing population of the core territory of the empire the Assyrians reclaimed plots of land to grow agricultural products, and the deportees were forced to till the Assyrian soil (Oded 1979; Becking 1992: 61-93; Aigner 2017; Wright and Elliott 2017: 457-61; Radner 2018; Sano 2020; Matarese 2021: 1-6.203-17; Cogan 2022: 174-75).

Deportations from the area of the former kingdom of Israel are mentioned in the Annals of Tiglath-Pileser III, the inscriptions of Sargon II and the Hebrew Bible. After the campaigns in 733–732 BCE, in which Tiglath-Pileser III conquered Damascus and annexed greater parts of Israel, he reports the deportation from at least four cities in the former Israelite territory. From [...]bara; Hannathon, Qa[...], [Yo]tbah, and the cities of Aruma and Merum captives were taken (TP III Slab from Kalhu = RINAP 1, 22:1′-7′; see Becking 1992: 15-16; Na'aman 1993: 104-106; Sano 2020: 195-99; Elayi 2022: 138-49). In a parallel account the king mentions the number of 13,520 captives exiled from Bīt-Ḫumrî and surroundings (TP III Slab from Kalhu = RINAP 1, 21:1′-11′; see Cogan 2022: 173). The damaged inscriptions mention numbers at three occasions, about 650 per city, which indicates that a few thousand Israelites were deported. The destination of the deportees is not given (Cogan 2021: 23). As mentioned above, Sargon II claims in the Nimrud Prism that he had:

31. [2]7,280 people, together with [their] chariots,
32. and the gods in whom they trusted, as spoil
33. I counted. Two-hundred chariots for [my] royal force
34. I collected from their midst.
35. The rest of them
36. I settled in the midst of Assyria

(Nimrud Prism IV = RINAP 2, 74: 31-36; see Gadd 1954; I disagree with Na'aman 2000, who on the assumption that there is a tendency to inflate the number of captives suggested that in the oldest version of the report the number was written as [4]7,280; with Cogan 2022: 173-74)

In another inscription, the slightly different number of 27,290 deportees is mentioned (Sargon II Display Inscription = RINAP 2, 7: 23-25; Becking 1992: 25-26; Na'aman 1993: 106-108; Radner 2018: 113-17; Sano 2020: 226-28; Valk 2020: 80). These numbers suggest an exact counting of the deported persons. Apart from the question whether the count was made at the start or at arrival, the numbers are difficult to control. Being part of Assyrian propaganda, the numbers given might be construed as an exaggeration of the reality (Faust 2021; Matarese 2021: 1-6, 203-17).

There are some glimpses of the fate of the deportees. Part of them were recruited for the Assyrian army, see for example the list of commanders in the Samarian cohort (CTN III 99 ii:16-23; Dalley and Postgate 1984: 177; Dezső 2006; Fales 2010: 117-40; Dezső 2012: 69-92; Dezső 2016: 17, 29-34; Radner 2018: 113-17; Sano 2020: 230; Cogan 2021: 30-32).

There are clear indications that the Assyrians offered an educational program to some selected deportees, mostly members of the local elites.

According to Parpola they 'received a thorough education in Assyrian literature, science and the ways of life in general' (Parpola 2003: 101-102). The final aim of this education was to prepare these selected deportees for a role at the Assyrian court or as loyal and reliable representatives of the central power in the Assyrian provinces and the client kingdoms (see Sano 2020: 63-72). Although some persons from the elite of various countries are mentioned in the documents, no reference to a deported Israelite is referred to in this context.

The majority would have been assigned to work at the newly reclaimed plots of land in the production of food. I will give an example. Documents name the Neo-Assyrian province of Ḫalaḫḫu—identical with biblical Halah mentioned in 2 Kgs 17:6; 18:11—as one of the destinies of the deportees. Israelite names were found: Aḫi-ia-qa-mu; Ba-ra-[ki]; and Ḫa-an-ni-i (ADD 755; see Becking 1992: 62-63). In a Neo-Assyrian letter it is stated:

> There is an estate of 4,000 hectares of arable land in a village called Qurani in the Halahhu province which the king my lord took and [gave] to the Nabû temple of Dur-Šarruken, and (in doing this) the king my lord [gave] this order to [Kiṣir]-Aššur: 'Give the Governor of the Land a village in return for the village [. . .]!' (SAA 1.106: 6-12)

I do not claim that the three deported Israelites just mentioned were working on this specific estate that had to produce for the Nabû temple—that is to feed the priests—but the context reveals their role in the chain of the agricultural economy.

One letter from the era of Sargon II makes clear that the Samarians in exile at times were summoned to perform corvée duties (elsewhere labelled *dullu*) to the king in assisting with the building of the new capital, Dur-Sharruken (Khorsabad):

> [As to ... concerning which the king], my lo[rd], wrote to me: '[Provi-] de [all the Sam]arians [in] your charge (with work) in Dur-Šarrukin' — I subsequently [sent (word) to] the sheikhs, [say]ing: 'Collect [all] the carpenters and potters; let them come and [direc]t the deportees [who are in D]ur-Šarrukin', but they did not agree to send them.
> [Sure]ly, [should I have sen]t [...] letters to the sheikhs, saying: '[If indeed you do not se]nd me craftsmen to work [for] me, [al]l [the people who are] here [. . .] upon you, [. . .] upon [. . .]', [they would have] promptly [se]nt [the craftsmen to] work [for me].
> Now (however), [following the king], my lo[rd]'s instructions, I strictly [. . .] do not argue with any [of the sheikhs].
> I have appointed [the carpenters and p]otters [. . .]
> [. . .] household utensils
> [. . . the king], my lord

[. . .] from
[. . . the Samari]ans
   (SAA 15: 280; see Radner 2018: 117-18)

The work for the new capital should be seen as an extra duty to the deported on top of their work on the estates, which would explain the reticence to perform the duty. This corvée was also imposed on deportees from other parts of the Assyrian Empire (Valk 2020: 84).

The fact that Israelite exiles could end up in debt is underscored by the following text:

> 3 homers of wheat according to the Judean seah (*ina* GIŠ.BÁN *ša* KUR.*ia-ú-di*), belonging to Aduni-ih'a, at the disposal of Attar-suri, servant of Padî
> He shall pay it in its original amount in the month of Elul in Nineveh.
> If he does not pay, it shall increase 5 seahs per homer.
> (r 4) Month Iyyar (II), (eponym year of) Gir-Ṣapunu.
> Witness Abi-ummi
> Witness Issar-tazi.
> Witness Bir-Šamaš
> 2 harvesters.
>   (ADD 149 = SAA 14, 77; see Zilberg 2016: 385-86)

The mention of the 'Judaean seah' (GIŠ.BÁN *ša* KUR.*ia-ú-di*) and the fact that Aduni-ih'a can be seen as an Israelite name indicate that an exile had entered dire straits.

These and other inscriptions indicate the presence of Israelite deportees throughout the Neo-Assyrian Empire. They, however do not reveal how these deported persons perceived and experienced their being in exile. There exists, however, one royal letter written by either Tiglath-Pileser III or Sargon II to the scribes Ashur-rimmani and Nabu-bel-ahheshu summoning them to take care of the deportees under their responsibility by taking good note of their health:

> If there is a sick person among the captives whom I send you from the empty-handed up to the needy, he is to be lifted up and placed in your care as long as he lives.
>   (ND 2735 = SAA 19: 6,9-14; Saggs 2001: 304-305; see Crouch 2009: 45-46; Younger 2015: 188; Sano 2020: 77-78).

It is unclear whether this summons is connected to deportees from Samerina. Whether or not those who were deported stayed in contact with those who remained in the territory of the former kingdom of Israel cannot be established.

The letter ABL 633 + k.11448 = CT 53, 46 = SAA 16, 63 should be construed as a report to King Esarhaddon from the 'Assyrian secret service' in Guzanu, the city that is explicitly mentioned in 2 Kgs 17.6 // 18.11 as one of the destinations of the Israelite deportees. The letter is written in order to inform the king about some crimes in Guzanu—especially a bribe leading to fraud with collected taxes—and about political turmoil between various local factions. Through the lines of the letter it becomes clear that the Assyrian power in the province of Guzanu was threatened and that the king had better be careful (see Fales 1981: 142-46). Among the informants are:

⌈p⌉*ni-ri-ia-u* LÚ.GAL NÍG.ŠID.MEŠ ᵖ*pal-ti-ia-u* ⌈LÚ⌉.[02]-*u*
Niri-Ia'u the chief of accounts, Palṭi-Ia'u the [depu]ty
    (SAA 16, 63: 4).

They are presented as trustworthy. This implies that at the provincial court in Guzanu, Samarians could rise to such a position (Radner 2018: 120-21). It should be noted that 'Halbišu the Samarian'—one of the informants to the king (SAA 16, 63: r.9) mentioned in the same document—has a Libyan name and can therefore not be seen as an Israelite (see Draper 2015: 3-4).

Another text that should be taken into account in this context is a legal text from Guzanu (StAT 2, 53; edition Draper 2015). The text documents the sale of a *tu-a-nu*, 'bath, bathhouse', by Sama', a Samarian, for fifty sheqel to Qišeraya. Among the many witnesses to this contract are two persons with Yahwistic names: Pal-liṭ-ya and Mi-zi-ya (Rev. 15-16). This document is evidence that Sama' had risen to such prosperity that he could own a bath(house) (Radner 2018: 119-20). At least for some, exile was more than hardship.

The repopulation of Samerina is mentioned in the Nimrud Prism:

37. I repopulated Samerina more than before.
38. People from countries, conquered by my hands
39. I brought in it.
    (Sargon II Nimrud Prism = RINAP 2,074: IV: 37-39; Faust 2021: 187-88; Na'aman 2016).

Although the phrasing of the lines just quoted is not standard in the reports of Neo-Assyrian conquests, the formula is attested several time in various constructions. After the conquest of the city of Ḫarḫar, for instance, it is stated in an inscription on the stone slabs from Room XIV in the palace at Khorsabad:

[I] brought there peop[le from the lands that I had conquered]
    (Sargon II Room XIV inscription = RINAP 2,04: 44'; see Oded 1979: 64).

This is a rather general phrase from which no historical conclusions can be drawn. Specific deportations to Samerina are only mentioned once in Neo-Assyrian inscriptions. In the Khorsabad Annals of Sargon II it is mentioned that:

> (As for) the Tamudu, [I]bādidi, Marsīma[ni], (and) Ḫayappa (tribes), faraway Arabs who live in the desert, did not know (either) overseer (or) commander, and had never brought their tribute to any king, I struck them down with the sword of the god Aššur, my lord, deported the remainder of them, and (re)settled (them) in the city Samaria.
> (Sargon II Annals from Khorsabad = RINAP II,001: 120-23; with a parallel in Sargon II Cylinder Inscription = RINAP II,043: 19-20; see Becking 1992: 32.102-104; Na'aman 1993: 108-12; Bagg 2010: 200-201; Faust 2021: 187-88)

Sargon II subjugated these tribes during a campaign to the Sinai-peninsula and the Egyptian border in *palû* 7 = 715 BCE. These tribes carried out the long-distance trade along the caravan routes, and Sargon probably wanted to strengthen his control over this trade. Numbers of deportees are not given in this text.

The Assyrians quite often depicted scenes of deportations on the walls in their palaces. These depictions had a double function. On the one hand they glorified the various kings and must have made a great impression on their subjects. On the other hand, these depictions were signs of warnings to the rulers of the client kingdoms or vassal states who came for an audience to the palace. The graphic scenes of Assyrian victory discouraged those vassals who were thinking about throwing off the Assyrian yoke. I will give one example of such a depiction, the deportation by Tiglath-Pileser III of inhabitants of Astoreth in which the gaze of the deportees expresses their sorrow (see Fig. 2):

In the Hebrew Bible, three short reports regarding the Assyrian deportation of people from the Northern Kingdom of Israel are given.

> In the time of Pekah king of Israel, Tiglath-Pileser king of Assyria came and took Ijon, Abel Beth Maacah, Janoah, Kedesh and Hazor. He took Gilead and Galilee, including all the land of Naphtali, and deported the people to Assyria (2 Kgs 15.29 ESV).

This note probably refers to the same event. In the biblical report on the conquest of Samaria, we find the note:

> In the ninth year of Hoshea, the king of Assyria captured Samaria, and he carried the Israelites away to Assyria and placed them in Halah, and on the Habor, the river of Gozan, and in the cities of the Medes. (2 Kgs 17.6 ESV)

It is unclear which Assyrian king is referred to in this verse. Most probably, Sargon II completed in 720 BCE the politics of Shalmaneser V, who had conquered Samaria but could not complete the endeavour due to his premature death in 722 (see Becking 1992; Cogan 2022: 170-73). The report is repeated in the next chapter:

FIGURE 2: King Tiglath-Pileser III of Assyria captures the city of Astartu. Pictured: An Assyrian soldier waving a mace escorts four deportees with sacks over their shoulders.
(From the Southwest Palace of Tiglath-Pileser III at Nimrud, ca. 730–727 BCE; British Museum; Elayi 2022: 138-46)

Shalmaneser king of Assyria came up against Samaria and besieged it, and at the end of three years he took it. In the sixth year of Hezekiah, which was the ninth year of Hoshea king of Israel, Samaria was taken. The king of Assyria carried the Israelites away to Assyria and put them in Halah, and on the Habor, the river of Gozan, and in the cities of the Medes. (2 Kgs 18.9-11 ESV).

This text seems to suggest that Shalmaneser was the king who ordered and carried out the deportations. Since no royal inscriptions of Shalmaneser V are known, this claim cannot be controlled. The inscriptions of Sargon II, on the other hand, make notice of the deportations in his reign. Assyrian documents make clear that Israelites were settled in the areas mentioned (Becking 1992: 62-63). It can be assumed, in my view, that in the short references to deportation in the book of Kings the memories of various events have been merged and conflated.

The repopulation of the area of the former Kingdom of Israel is mentioned in the book of Kings:

> And the king of Assyria brought people from Babylon, Cuthah, Avva, Hamath, and Sepharvaim, and placed them in the cities of Samaria instead of the people of Israel. And they took possession of Samaria and lived in its cities. (2 Kgs 17.24 ESV; see Sano 2020: 228-29)

It should be noted that the author of the book of Kings does not provide numbers. No quantity of deported persons or of persons brought in are given. Information on the quality of life of all these persons is absent. The book of Kings does not give information on the question whether life in exile or life in the conquered territory was full of hardship or of prosperity.

There might be one textual glimpse on the reality. In 2 Kgs 17.25-27, it is narrated that YHWH had sent lions to the territory as a punishment for the fact that the new settlers did not worship him but continued the religion they took with them. It is, of course, difficult to construct history on the basis of the rather theological statement. But it might be defensible to see the note as a clue to the reality in the final decades of the eighth century BCE. I would propose to read this lion incident from the perspective of climate change.

Climate is not constant. The eighth century BCE was a period of change. Up to 700, the global temperature was rising. The data from the Greenland Ice Sheet project show a decline of temperature after 700 (Meese et al. 1994). This implies that in the last decade of the eighth century lack of rainfall would have influenced negatively the agrarian production and that after 700 the circumstances changed for the better. Droughts could well have been the reason for the impoverishing of farmers. A warmer climate often causes bubonic plagues. This has been the case in mediaeval Europe, but also in 707 BCE. There is evidence that in that year a *mūtāmu*, Akkadian for 'deadly disease' (*CAD* M/2, 296-97), scourged the Assyrian Empire (see SAA 1.171:14; 1.180:10'-12'; Babylonian Chronicle I ii:5; Gallagher 1999: 267-68). Such an epidemic could have had a destructive effect on agriculture in weakening the resilience of the production of food. The dendrochronological data from the ancient Near East in that period show a comparable pattern: before 700 less biomass and after 700 increasingly more (Pearson and Stuiver 1986). This drought could have been the cause of the migration of lions. When the food supply in their original habitat diminishes, lions go adrift in search of food (Tuqa et al. 2014). The drought in combination with the forced migrations most probably was one of the main factors for the depopulation of the province Samerina as brought to light by the archaeological evidence (see Faust 2015: 767-74; 2021: 73-83).

The other important factor for the decrease of the population in the former Kingdom of Israel might have been a disbalance between deportees and settlers (thus Valk 2020: 88-90). This assumption is difficult to control in view of the fact that only a few times numbers are given in the evidence. It would, however, explain the scarcity of the population and the relative poverty of the area.

3.2.3 *Paying Taxes and their Problems*

In the Nimrud Prism of Sargon II (see above 2.2.2), it is stated that after the conquest of Samaria, the population of the newly established province is now considered as people from Assyria:

37. I repopulated Samerina more than before.
38. People from countries, conquered by my hands
39. I brought in it. My commissioner
40. I appointed as governor over
41. I counted them as Assyrians.
  (Sargon II Nimrud Prism = RINAP II,074: IV: 37-41).

This phrase is attested rather frequently in Neo-Assyrian inscriptions. In a text parallel to the Nimrud Prism, this line is phrased alternatively:

> GUN LÚ.GAL *maḫ-re-e e-mid-su-nu-ti*
> I imposed upon them (the same) tribute (as) the former king (had paid)
>   (Sargon II Display Inscription = RINAP II,7; 24-25; see also Sargon II Annals = RINAP II, 1: 17; Yamada 2022: 281).

In other words, the Assyrian citizenship of the inhabitants of the province—settlers and remainders alike—implied the yearly paying of GUN (*biltu*). This noun could refer both to the 'yield, produce' of a field and to the 'tax, tribute' to be paid (*CAD* B: 229-36).

In this same Great Display Inscription of Sargon II the phrase *u sittute inūšunu ušāḫiz* occurs (Sargon II Display Inscription = RINAP II, 7:24). This phrase is traditionally rendered with 'and *allowed* the remainder to *practice* their (normal) *occupations*' (Becking 1992: 26; RINAP II). Aster suggested that the phrase should be translated as 'I trained the remnant in their crafts'. This would imply that those inhabitants of the former Northern Kingdom who were not exiled to Assyria received an extra training in order to be productive for the Empire. The Assyrians would like to receive a substantial yearly tribute (Aster 2019: 602-608). Cogan, however, correctly argued that the word *šittu*, 'remnant, remainder', in various Neo-

Assyrian inscriptions does refer to a group of people next to the specifically mentioned persons going into exile, as chariot drivers for instance, who too were deported. The inscription of Sargon mentioned refers to deported Samarians, not those who had avoided deportation. Besides, he construes the expression *inūšunu ušāḫiz* to mean 'I allowed them to hold, exercise their technical craft'. In other words, the phrase under consideration indicates that various craftsmen were deported to Assyria (Cogan 2022: 179-82). This implies that the workforce in Samerina was reduced in favor of the economy of the core of the Assyrian Empire.

In the Neo-Assyrian system of taxation a difference was made between the incorporated provinces and client kingdoms of the vassals. For clarity's reason, I follow the often-made distinction between 'tax' and 'tribute' (Kerekes 2011; Faust 2021: 14). Provinces had to pay taxes in kind—mainly corn and straw—while vassals were supposed to send tribute in the form of luxury goods. See, for instance, the tribute paid by Hezekiah to Sennacherib:

> In addition to the thirty talents of gold and eight hundred talents of silver, gems, antimony, jewels, AN.ZA.GUL.ME-stones, ivory-inlaid couches, ivory-inlaid chairs, elephant hides, elephant tusks, ebony, boxwood, all kinds of valuable treasures, as well as his daughters, his harem, his male and female musicians, which he had brought after me to Nineveh, my royal city. To pay tribute and to accept servitude, he dispatched his messengers. (Senn Rassam Cylinder = RINAP III,004: 55-58; see Bär 1996: 51-52)

The duties for an Assyrian province could be fourfold (see Faust 2021: 17-18):

1. Some taxes had to be paid in kind, mainly straw and corn. The purpose of these taxes was to feed the Assyrian administration and its horses. Part of the taxes remained in the province and the other part was shipped to the core of the empire, although this was too expensive for the province of Samerina in view of the distance to Assur and the costs of overland transport (see Postgate 1974: 189; Kerekes 2011; Faust 2021: 17).
2. In various provinces, the Assyrians implemented the *gin(n)û*-system. The noun *gin(n)û* refers to the regular offerings. In Neo-Assyrian times the provisions for the fixed offerings for the Aššur temple in the city of Assur were supposed to be supplied in turn by the Assyrian provinces (Postgate 1974: 214-16; Holloway 2002: 67-68, 100-108). This implies that the inhabitants of an area had to pay to the Assyrian temple built in the capital of the province in order to sustain the priests involved in that temple (Kerekes 2011: 107).

3. The provinces were also supposed to supply non-material duties in the form of 'intelligence', by warning the Assyrian power about possible rebellions (Kerekes 2011: 108; on the Assyrian secret service see Spieckermann 1982: 307-12; Dubovský 2006).
4. Occasionally, the inhabitants of a province had to pay a special tax to the governor (see Kerekes 2011: 106-107).

On a list of incoming tribute of 'red wool and madder', the provinces of [... Sam]aria and Megiddo are mentioned among the areas who delivered these goods (SAA 7, 116:1.6; see Cogan 2021: 45).

One Neo-Assyrian letter shows that the paying of the corn tax was not always easy:

> A letter from Arihu to Nabû-duri-uṣur. Good health to my lord!
> As to the corn tax of the Samarians, my lord should send a notice whether it exists or not, and let us be content with that. The officials are passive, they keep where they are, they don't go to do their work, nor can we give them orders.
> I have been petitioning you since last year until now in this very manner about the income, but we have not brought in any income whatever. Now send a notice whether it exists or not!
>   (ABL 1201 = SAA 1, 220; see Postgate 1974: 182; Becking 1992: 107-108; Dezső 2016: 122).

Arihu was most probably an Assyrian officer responsible for the control of the incoming taxes (he is also mentioned in SAA 1, 261). In quite diplomatic words he inquires of Nabû-duri-uṣur about the absence—read: non-delivery—of the ŠE.*nu-sa-ḫi*, 'corn tax', from the province of Samerina (on this word see Postgate 1974: 174-99; Dezső 2016: 121-12). In polite language he urges Nabû-duri-uṣur to deliver the tax. Although mentioned in three other Neo-Assyrian letters his function is unclear (SAA 1, 10; 215; 221). The current letter can be read as an indication that the corn tax must have been a heavy duty for the impoverished province (Aster and Faust 2015: 204-207; Faust 2021: 193-94).

As for the *gin(n)û*-system, there are no indications that this system was implemented in the province of Samerina. The same is true for the third and fourth elements. The absence of evidence, however, is not evidence for the fact that from the province of Samerina no intelligence reports were sent or special taxes for the governor were collected. We just do not know.

The client states, or vassal kingdoms, were supposed to bring a yearly tribute to Assyria. This tribute consisted mainly in luxury goods (see Bär 1996; Radner 2007; Mattila 2018). Two examples. First, the list of goods that were brought from, *inter alii*, the city of Ashkelon:

> 1 horse, 1 mare, total 2 in Guzana;
> 1 mare 1 year old foal in Nisibin, total 4;
> total 28 horses (from) Askelon (KUR*Iš-qa-lu-na-a*)
> ...
> ... talents of silver, yearly tribute.
> 40 mana of silver ...;
> 1 talent of silver paid for grain, total 3 talents 40 mana,
> 20 lengths of linen cloth, 50 pieces of decorated harness cloth, total
> 70 lengths of ... cloth
>   (ND 2672:1-24; ed. Parker 1961: 42; see Na'aman 2004: 58)

This yearly tribute could only be paid when the economy in the client states was flourishing, as is also indicated by archaeological excavations that indicate a blossoming in the time of King Manasseh (Finkelstein 1994). The fact that no complaints regarding the non-payment of these tributes are known can be seen as an indication that in fact the southwestern client kingdoms were able to yield the tribute and that the duties did not impoverish the area. The question must be asked, however, who profited from the economic blossoming? I will come to that later (3.2.5). Second, a report of Marduk Remami to King Sargon on tribute brought by emissaries of vassal states to Kalhu:

> I have received 45 horses of the [pala]ce. The emissaries from Egypt, Gaza, Judah, Moab and Ammon entered Calah on the 12th with their tribute. The 24 horses of the (king) of Gaza are with him. The Edomite, [Ashdo]dite and Ekronite [. . .].
>   (SAA 1.110: Rev. 4-13; see Zilberg 2016: 390-91; Cogan 2021: 57-59; see Na'aman 2004: 58; May 2022a: 189)

The payment of this yearly tribute does not seem to have been problematic for Judah. The same is true for the delivery of a tribute in silver from Ekron, as documented in a shipment record from the early reign of Sennacherib:

> 1 talent (of silver measured) by the royal light (talent). Padî, the ruler of Ekron.
> Month of Arahsamna (VIII), 23rd day, eponym year of Bel-šarrani.
>   (SAA 11.50)

3.2.4 The 'Heavy Yoke' of ilku and dullu

The systems of *ilku* and *dullu* were Neo-Assyrian instruments that regulated the obligation of corvée for the inhabitants of their provinces and vassal states. They are the Assyrian equivalents of a system that lasted worldwide deep into the early modern age as parts of the feudal system.

Tenant farmers, for example, not only had to pay the lease in kind and or money but could be forced to work a few days a year on the estate of the landowner. These duties existed in acts such as tilling the soil of the estate, harvesting on the estate in favor of the landowner, repair work on roads and fences (Bloch 1949; Yamada 2022: 280-81). Comparable systems of forced labor were present in ancient Israel as well as in the entire ancient Near East (Morgenstern 1962; Jenei 2019). In the Hebrew Bible, such an obligation to work is not rejected per se. The duties imposed by Solomon are, however, assessed as a token of royal abuse of power (1 Kgs 4–12). A letter written to Sargon II indicates that not all people in Assyria were happy with these duties:

> Now, people have taken fright at the *ilku*-service of the king their lord and [are grumbling]: 'Why are they [persecuting] us month after month?' They keep escaping one after the other and are settling in the district of Arpad, beyond the River.
> (SAA 1.183: 12-17; see Valk 2020: 83-84)

The Assyrian noun *ilku*, 'services performed for a higher authority in turn for land held', refers to a variety of activities in favor of the owner of the land by the tenant (*CAD* I/J: 73-83; Postgate 1974: 63-93; Spieckermann 1982: 314-15; Desző 2016: 55-57). They range from payment in kind to military services and building activities. The almost synonymous noun *dullu*, lit. 'hardship', refers to a variety of forced labor, corvée work all in service to the crown (*CAD* D: 173-74). Since the inhabitants of the Assyrian provinces were 'counted as Assyrians', the people in the province of Samerina could be summoned for these duties.

Evidence for this forced labor in the province of Samerina, however, is hard to find. There are—as yet—no documents related to Samerina in which the nouns *ilku* and *dullu* occur.

There is a court-order found in a cuneiform inscription from Samaria that reads as follows

> [W]hen Nergal-shallim gives a command on the tenth day of the month Ab, then Aja-Ahhe shall give to the city-counsellor 6 oxen and 12 + x donkeys.
> (Postgate 1974: 59; Becking 1992: 112-13)

The ordered delivery of the animals might be part of an *ilku*-duty.

One Assyrian text can be interpreted as a report on corvée work. In a report on the progress of the building of the new palace of Sargon II in Dur-Sharruken it is written:

> [He said: 'The re]st of the work that I am doing [is . . . ; I have receiv-] ed from him [x] bricks, but he is still glazing [the kiln-fired bricks]'.

I am [herewith] sending [the . . .]s of the br[ickwork o]f his wall (assignment) [to the king], my lord.
[Perhaps the ki]ng, my lord, will say: '[To who]m have [you] given bricks [. . .]?'
[40,000] to (the governor of) Arpad, [40,000 t]o (the governor of) Sama[ria, 40,000 to] (the governor of) Megid[do], in all [1]20,000 (bricks taken) from the king's entourage.
[In all 30,000 f]rom Na'di-ilu.
[All told], I have given out [1]50,000 bricks; [but] I have omitted the bricks of the royal village managers [about which the ki]ng, my lord, wrote me.
[The ki]ng, my lord, knows that the eunuchs and the royal entourage from [whom] I have been taking the bricks which I have given [to] the magnates are going to petition the king. The king, my [lo]rd, may do as he deems best; [the ki]ng, my [lo]rd, knows that [I have] in the past [days given brick]s to the ki[ng's] entourage.
(SAA 5, 291: 6-rev13; see Becking 1992: 111-12; Valk 2020: 84-86; Cogan 2021: 45-46)

The brickmaking must have been done on site either by deportees or by persons still living in the provinces who were conscripted for this duty (Cogan 2021: 45-46). It can, therefore, be assumed that the local population in the province was on occasion summoned to perform duties for the Assyrians in building or road construction.

According to a list from around 700, the client kingdom of Judah paid 10 minas of silver (*ABL* 632 = SAA 11,50:5-6; see Zilberg 2016: 388-89). The character of this donation is, however, unclear.

3.2.5 *Economic Uprising around Ekron, but Cui Bono?*

Above (2.2.2), I have argued—adopting the analysis of Faust—that the olive oil industry at Ekron was part of a greater economic scheme. This scheme was organized around the harbor city of Ashkelon. It supplied goods for the Philistine/Phoenician maritime trade and gave rise to an economic blossoming in the Philistine coastal area, the Shephelah, and the client kingdom of Judah (Faust and Weiss 2005, 2012; Faust 2008; 2011; 2015: 765-77; 2021: 116-38; Maeir, Welch and Eniukhina 2021). Different from the situation in the province of Samaria, the Judaean territory did not—in general—suffer from the Neo-Assyrian presence.

The question, however, should be asked: Who profited? Economic blossoming generally does not lead to a fair and equal distribution of wealth among the inhabitants of the area involved. Human history is full of examples that show that the growth of an economy mostly lead to a distinction between the 'have much' and the 'have less'. A relatively rich elite is always able to gather more fruits from the tree of wealth than the commoners in a society.

Whether this discrepancy in wealth also existed in the southwestern client kingdoms during the Assyrian age is not easy to establish. There are, however, three pieces of evidence that speak in its favor. (1) At Ashkelon a very international repertoire of earthenware was found, indicating the wealth of some of its inhabitants (Master 2003); (2) in the city of Ekron, a few elite zones have been uncovered (Faust 2021: 117); (3) the list of goods brought as a tribute from Ashkelon is indicative of the wealth of the harbor city. Since no comparable evidence has been found in the territory of Judah, I hesitate to expand this view over the client kingdom around Jerusalem.

There are, however, two topics that might substantiate such a view. Above, I have paid attention to a line in the book of Zephaniah, where inhabitants of Judah and Jerusalem are rebuked:

> I shall punish the officials and the king's sons,
>   and all who clothe themselves in foreign attire. (Zeph. 1:8)

I agree with Christoph Uehlinger, who argues that dressing in foreign attire of leading persons in Jerusalem is an act of breaking the social code by accepting the foreign as more important than the local. It should be seen as a mimetic act of the local elite to the culture of the greater power that Assyria was (Uehlinger 1996; Sweeney 2003: 85; for a different view see Berlin 1994: 78). As said, it cannot be decided whether this trend was imposed by the Assyrians or just another form of local adaptation of the international trend.

This dressing according to the foreign fashion can be seen in parallel with the imitation of the Assyrian Palace Ware. The local elite modelled their tableware after the example of the Assyrians in order to show that they had transcended the suburban provinciality (see Na'aman and Thareani-Sussely 2006; Faust 2021: 162-66). These adaptations were as such relatively harmless. When, however, the Assyrian culture was more and more construed as oppressive they became symbols of collaboration and expressions of a baleful mindset.

3.3 Never Analyse the Absent Patient but Take the Memory Seriously

When I was training to become a pastor in the Dutch Reformed Church, the phrase 'never analyse the absent patient' passed by. It was a warning for us—future pastors—not to rely on stories about a person but always make contact with the person him/herself. Over the gap of ages, it is impossible to diagnose the inhabitants of Judah and Israel with regard to possible trauma during the Assyrian age. Nevertheless, a cautious estimation can be made on the basis of the evidence discussed above.

The evidence gathered here indicates that the period of the Assyrian occupation was full of hardship for the inhabitants of the province of Samerina, but less for those who lived in the client kingdom of Judah. As for those in exile, the majority suffered from being in a strange land, while some were able to reach important positions in the Assyrian economy and administration. The main misery was the fact that they could not live in their own land (as summarized by Carr 2014: 20-38).

Any individual case could be softened as a personal difficulty or woven away by the pseudo-wisdom such as 'where chopping is done chips fall'. The cumulation of all cases, however, makes clear that they cannot be construed as mere collateral facts of life. In the perception of those who suffered, they were experienced as life-limiting and happiness-confining examples of trauma.

3.4 The Traumatic Experience

All in all, a nuanced picture of the 'Assyrian yoke' emerged from the existing evidence. Although there was more black than white, the period cannot entirely be summarized in the words misery and alienation. It should be noted, however, that like the adjective *rā'* in Nah. 3.19, the words 'trauma' and 'traumatic' have an evaluative dimension. What I mean to say is that the Assyrian period was experienced as traumatic. The trauma was not balanced by occasional moments of joy. The period of Assyrian rule has been imprinted as traumatic in the collective memory of the inhabitants of the vassal kingdom of Judah as well as of the province Samerina and by those exiled to Assyria (on the concept of collective memory, see Assmann 1988). They all had a 'shared mental representation' of the Assyrian age as a (mostly) traumatic period (Volkan 1998: 41). The author of the book of Nahum reacts to and reflects on this collective memory in order to help the communities to cope with the implied trauma. In that way by opening the silence, the author is taking their memory seriously. His use of the word *rā'*, 'evil', refers to a trans-generationally built-up meta-narrative that assesses the Assyrian age negatively while overlooking and/or silencing the positive moments of that period.

After a look at the perennial history of traumatic events, I will turn to the book of Nahum and read the ancient text as an answer to trauma.

4

Trauma Continued (the History of Humankind)

At first, it was my intention to produce a series of images reflecting various kinds of trauma brought upon human beings. In view of copyright problems, I changed my mind. Below follows an incomplete list of traumatic events during the history of humankind. The enumeration might seem sober and stark, almost without emotion. Behind the listed items, however, lies a gaping abyss of misery and brokenness. This is a far from complete depiction of the *si-mu la-zu*, 'unhealing wound' (Gula-curse, SAA 2 § 52) inflicted on our body, soul, and community.

	1200	Bronze Age Collapse	
1	ninth century BCE	Conquest of Upumu by Shalmanassar III I filled the wide plain with the corpses of his warriors.... These [rebels] I impaled on stakes. ...A pyramid (pillar) of heads I erected in front of the city.	Kurkh Monolith
2	587	Fall of Jerusalem to the Babylonians	2 Kings 25
3	332 BCE	Massacre of Tyre, Alexander the Great	Arrian, *Anabasis* 2.24.4-5
4	150 BCE	Judith beheading Holoferness	Judith 13.9
5	70 CE	Titus's conquest of Jerusalem	Flavius Josephus, *War of the Jews*, 6.9.3.
6	451	Atrocities by Attila the Hun at the Battle of Chalons	

7	455	Vandals Plunder Rome	Procopius, 'The Vandalic War' in *The History of the Wars*, Books III & IV.
8	1095–1291	Cruelty of the Crusades	
9	1300–1500	Black Death Pandemics	
10	1302	Guldensporenslag (Battle of the Golden Spurs)	
11	1389	Battle at the Blackbird Field in Kosovo	
12	1415	Battle of Agincourt	
13	1566	Iconoclasm in the Netherlands	
14	1576	Spanish Fury at Antwerp	
15	1620	The Battle at White Mountain (Bila Hora) Fought near Prague	
16	1641	Irish Catholic Forces in the Rebellion Were Accused of Ripping Open Pregnant Women	
17	1650–1850	Slave Trade by Westerners	
18	1755	Great Lisbon Earthquake	
19	1803–1815	Napoleontic Wars	
20	1817	Battle at Chacabuco, Chilean Independence War	
21	1845–1852	*an Gorta Mór*; Irish Potato Famine	
22	1860–1865	American Civil War	
23	1880–1881	First Boer War; Eerste Vryheidsoorlog	
24	1883	Eruption of the Krakatau Volcano	
25	1890	Wounded Knee Massacre	
26	1914–1918	Trenches in Flanders and France	
27	1915–1916	Gallipoli Campaign - Çanakkale Savaşı	Eric Bogle, 'And the Band Played Waltzing Matilda'
28	1918–1920	Spanish Flu	
29	1930–1955	Главное управление исправительно-трудовых лагерей (GULAG)	

30	1937	Nanjing Massacre	
31	1937	Bombing of Guernica	Picasso Painting
32	1940	Germans Bombing London, Coventry, Rotterdam …	
33	1940–1945	Auschwitz, Sobibor, Theresianstadt …	
34	1941	Pearl Harbor Attack	
35	1944	Oradour-sur-Glane Massacre	
36	1945	Bombing of Dresden by the RAF	
37	1945	Atomic Bombs on Hiroshima and Nagasaki	
38	1952	Northsea Flood, England, Belgium, Netherlands	
39	1961	Massacre in Sharpeville, South Africa	
40	1968	My Lai, Vietnam	
41	1975–1979	Killing Fields Cambodia	
42	1981	HIV/Aids	
43	1994	Genocide in Rwanda	
44	1996–2008	Civil Wars in Eastern Congo	
45	2001	Масакр у Сребрениџи Srebrenica Massacre	
46	2001	Attack on the WTC, 9/11	
47	2004	Indian Ocean Earthquake and Tsunami	
48	2020	Corona Pandemic	
49	2022	Russian Invasion in Ukraine	
50	2022	Shooting at the Robb Elementary School in Uvalde, Texas	
51	2023	Oct. 7th Operation Al Aqsa storm: Hamas attacks military bases, schools and kibbutzim in Israel. Answered by Israelian attacks on Gaza and Raphia	
A	Perennial	Rape and Sexual Abuses	

5

The Book of Nahum: Composition and Date

The book of Nahum in the Hebrew Bible counts only 558 words in its three chapters. The book of Obadiah alone is shorter in this collection of ancient texts. This limited size, however, does not imply the absence of exegetical problems in Nahum. The lengthy list of scholarly work on the Minor Prophet is witness to that. I will note a few problematic questions:

1. Can the book be read as a unified composition?
2. Do we have to accept a series of redactional layers in the book?
3. How does Nahum relate to the assumed growth of the corpus of the minor prophets?
4. When was Nahum written—the first draft and the final composition?
5. Can the book be construed as texts predicting the fall of Nineveh?
6. Or does Nahum originate after that event, and is the book as a whole to be read as a *vaticinium ex eventu*?
7. The beginning of ch. 1 clearly contains an, albeit incomplete, acrostic on the Hebrew alphabet. How far does this acrostic extend, and is it appropriate to restore a complete alphabet? (for a discussion, see, e.g., Floyd 1994; Baumann 2005: 52-60; Christensen 2009: 209-16; Jeremias 2019: 54-59; Noegel 2021: 218-29)
8. Which persons are addressed with the 'you-forms' in 1.9–2.3?
9. What is the connection between ch. 1 and the rest of the book?
10. How do we cope with a God who is presented as both revengeful and condoning?

It is not my purpose to present a thorough discussion of all these questions—if that were only possible. I will present my own view substantiated with argument.

I read the book of Nahum as a literary and conceptually coherent text. Nahum functioned as a minority pamphlet written in the final decades of the waning Assyrian power. It functioned as a consoling letter to all 'over whom the Assyrian evil had come constantly'. It supported the political faction in Jerusalem that wanted to get rid of the Assyrian yoke. Yet, the pamphlet is not an appeal to use human power against a world power crumbling apart. Liberation is seen as an act of Yhwh in favor of all those who suffered (see Becking 1977, 1995).

5.1 The Composition of Nahum

In my view, the book of Nahum consists—after the superscription in 1.1—of four elements (see also Sweeney 1992, 1995; Spronk 1997; Bosman 2002: 590-91; Tuell 2016):

	Verses	Contents	Remarks
A	1.2-8	A hymn to Yhwh	Presenting: • Salvation for some [a] • Doom for others [b]
B	1.9-14	Elaboration and application of unit A	
C	2.1-3	The forthcoming salvation for Judah and the exiles	Identifying [a]
D	2.4–3.19	The forthcoming doom for Assyria	Identifying [b]
D.1	2.4-14	Description of the assault on Nineveh	
D.2	3.1-7	*Woe*-oracle and a word of judgement	
D.3	3.8-19	Description of the downfall of Nineveh	Its fate is compared with that of Thebes in Egypt that was conquered by the Assyrians

I am aware of the fact that there are other proposals to delimit the units of the book of Nahum (e.g. Seybold 1989; Roberts 1991: 37-38; O'Brien 2002, 2004: 23-25; Christensen 2009: 41-51; Jeremias 2019). My proposal takes account of as many features as possible, such as poetic structures, compositional signs, and the delimitation markers in the ancient manuscripts (see also Spronk 1995, 1997; Timmer 2020). I will give some primary remarks on these units.

5.1.1 *A Hymn to YHWH*

This hymn is molded in the form of concentric symmetry (see Douglas 2007). It contains three sub-units (see also De Vries 1966: 477-79):

A.1   1.2-3a   God's anger and long suffering
A.2   1.3b-6   God's theophany leading to judgment
A.1'   1.7-8   God as saviour and destroyer.

In the first textual unit, a condensed hymnic theology is given (A.1). In seven cola, seven 'attributes' of God are presented. In the middle part—A.2—the appearance of God in lyrical images is given. The language of this sub-unit is rather traditional. In Nah. 1.6 the theophany ends in an unspecific way with a question: 'Who can stand firm before his fury?' A comparable question is absent in other descriptions of a theophany in the Hebrew Bible or in ancient Near Eastern texts (on the literary form of a theophany see Jeremias 1965; Scriba 1995; DeLapp 2018). The final sub-unit describes two polar 'attributes' of God: his goodness and his destroying power.

These three sub-units have different literary backgrounds. A.1 reflects the twofold testimony from the traditional creed in Exod. 34.6-7:

> The LORD, the LORD, the compassionate and gracious God,
> slow to anger, abounding in love and faithfulness,
> maintaining love to thousands, and forgiving wickedness, rebellion and sin.
> Yet he does not leave the guilty unpunished;
> he punishes the children and their children for the sin of the parents
> to the third and fourth generation. (Exod. 34.6-7 NIV)

A.2 is rooted in the language of the theophany, while A.1' has connections with the language of confidence and judgment. Nevertheless, they form a literary and conceptually coherent unit. This coherence can be phrased as follows: God is coming to give a judgment in a crisis in history since he is a jealous God. In the ordeal, YHWH will be a shelter for some but a destroyer for others (A.1').

By implication, this opening unit contains some starting points for threads that pass through the whole of the composition. The book of Nahum is an example of the literary technique of 'slowly unfolding' (see Beek 1948: 133). The practical meaning of the traditional language in the opening hymn becomes steadily clear in the prophetic announcements of salvation and doom (elements B and D).

5.1.2 Elaboration and Application

At first sight, the unit Nah. 1.9-14 has an enigmatic character. The texts seem to be in disorder. Wellhausen proposed the idea that in this unit two originally independent traditions have been conflated, leading to a text without a clear meaning (Wellhausen 1963: 160). Various scholars have followed this lead, although they mutually demarcate the original texts different (Jeremias 1970: 20-21; Schulz 1973: 15-21, 24; Seybold 1989: 68-73; Nogalski 1993a: 111-15). Jakob Wöhrle has argued that the unit should be read as an oracle against the Judaean people (Wöhrle 2008: 24-39; 2018: 540).

In reaction to these proposals and as a starting point for their refusal, it should be noted that in this unit the genus of the second-person pronouns and pronominal suffixes changes:

	Second person forms in Nahum 1.9-14	
9	$t^e\text{ḥašš}^e b\hat{u}n$ 'you plot'	2.m.pl.
11	$mimm\bar{e}k$ 'from you'	2.f.s.
12	$w^e\text{'innitik}$ 'and I have afflicted you'	2.f.s.
	$^{ta}\text{'annēk}$ 'I will (no longer) afflict you'	2.f.s.
13	$m\bar{e}\text{'ālāyik}$ 'from you'	2.f.s.
	$\hat{u}m\hat{o}srotayik$ 'your shackles'	
14	'ālêkā 'against you'	2.m.s.
	$mišš imkā$ 'from your name (= family tree)'	2.m.s.
	$^{,e}loh\hat{e}k\bar{a}$ 'your gods'	2.m.s.
	$qibr^ek\bar{a}$ 'your grave'	2.m.s.
	$qall\hat{o}t\bar{a}$ 'you are contemptible'	2.m.s.

Already a superficial reading of the unit 1.9-14 makes clear that the destinies of the 'masculine' and the 'feminine' you-characters are different. The feminine-you will meet liberation. She will no longer be afflicted, and the shackles of her servitude will be broken (Timmer 2021: 160). The masculine-you will be cut out from history. His grave is already prepared. I therefore agree with De Vries that the different forms refer to different groups, although I do not share beforehand his conclusion that the different forms would refer to Judah (feminine) and Nineveh (masculine) (De Vries 1966: 480; Sweeney 1992: 370-72; Lanner 2006: 81-82; Timmer 2020: 99; Wessels 2020: 339-40). In my view, the slowly unfolding of the message of Nahum will only later in the book reveal the identity of both groups.

Nevertheless this second unit clarifies some elements from the first unit. The lofty lyrics on God's jealousy, wrath and goodness are now reified into forthcoming but concrete categories such as liberation and destruction. The question of which fate would affect which group will have to wait until the next sections.

5.1.3 *The Forthcoming Salvation for Judah and the Exiles*

This short unit is composed in two sets with a comparable structure: Introduction—summons—motivation of the summons:

2.1	Intr	See on the mountains
		    the feet of the messenger
		        announcing peace.

	Imp	Celebrate, Judah, your feasts! Pay your vows!
	Mot	Because it will no longer happen that the Wicked One (Belial) will pass through you. He is eliminated completely!
2.2	Intr	The scattered one will come up to you.

	Imp	Look out from your lookout-station!
		    Keep watch over the road!
		Strengthen the loins!
		    Make firm with abundant power!

2.3	Mot	Because YHWH returns
		    with the pride of Jacob, which is the pride of Israel,
		Since destroyers have destroyed them
		    and their protectors are devastated.[1]

This unit gives a clear answer to the question of which group will be the receiver of the liberation? The salvation will come in two dimensions. On the one hand, Judah will be liberated from the 'Wicked One'; and on the other, the exiles from Israel are promised a return to their own land.

5.1.4 *The Forthcoming Doom for Assyria*

The description of the fate of Nineveh is molded in a concentric symmetry:

D.1	2.4-14	Description of the assault on Nineveh
D.2	3.1-7	*Woe*-oracle and a word of judgment
D.1'	3.8-19	Description of the downfall of Nineveh.

---

1. Notes on the translation will be given below in 6.2.

Like two side panels in a triptych, the military descriptions of the downfall of Nineveh flank the central part that functions as the deeper motivation of the forthcoming doom. In other words: God's judgment and not human ideas of revenge are seen as the deeper cause of the destruction.

5.1.4.1 Description of the Assault on Nineveh

This unit is presented as a threat to the masculine 'you-character'. The unit consists in three sub-units. The first of them, 2.4-8, is written in veiled language. In the quickly alternating images of war and combat no name is given. What is described are the military images such as the 'shield of his warriors' or 'stumbling officers'. The sum of the fragments presents an image of total destruction not unlike the scenes of conquest on the reliefs in the Assyrian palaces. In this first sub-unit it remains unclear who will bite in the dust of disaster.

The second sub-unit, 2.9-13, reveals the name of the city whose fate is sealed: $nîn^ewēh$, 'Nineveh'. From the days of Sennacherib until its downfall in 612 BCE, Nineveh was the glorious capital of the Neo-Assyrian Empire. The unit refers to two symbols of the power of the city: (a) the splendid waterworks and (b) the den of marauding lions. Both will find their end.

The final, albeit shortest, subunit, 2.14, contains a menacing prophecy introduced with formulaic words: $hin^enî\ 'ēlayik$, 'Behold, I am against you' (*Herausforderungsformel;* see Humbert 1933). This verse underscores the view that the downfall of Nineveh should be construed as a divine act and not purely as a human political event.

Within the composition of the book of Nahum, the unit 2.4-14 makes clear the identity of the group who is to receive the horror of divine wrath.

5.1.4.2 *Woe*-Oracle and a Word of Judgment

The unit 3.1-7 consists of two parts: after a *woe*-oracle (3.1-4), a menacing prophecy of judgment introduced with formulaic words $hin^enî\ 'ēlayik$ is placed (3.5-7).The unit builds up to the degrading rhetorical question 'Where can I seek comforters for you?' (3.7c).

The first sub-unit is composed as a woe-oracle. With this genre a person or a group is bewailed beforehand. The genre elaborates on the mourning cry with which a dead person is bewailed after dying. In applying this form to the living, an author classifies the life of a person or a group as having turned their life in a dead-end-street: a mourning cry will be their inevitable fate (Westermann 1964: 137-42; ET 1991; Janzen 1972; Hoyt 2019: 158-61). A woe-oracle traditionally is built up in three elements: address—accusation—announcement. The address indicates the person(s) who will be bewailed: the city of blood (3.1-3). The accusation contains a list of wrongdoings and trespasses that form the reason for the punishment (3.4). The announcement is described in the second sub-unit (3.5-7).

Using the participles characteristic for this genre, the address displays an image of all thing that happened in Nineveh. The military exploits—horses, chariots and swords—do not refer to the way in which Nineveh will be destroyed but display daily life in Assyria. Nineveh is depicted as a city that is the centre of military atrocities and economic abuse (see also Van der Woude 1977; 1978: 113-16).

The preposition *min* in *mērob z*^{e}*nûnê zônā* has causal force and hence introduces the accusation (Dahood 1971; Cathcart 1973a: 129). Nineveh is *woe*-ed because of her acts as seductress and sorceress. These are evaluative terms for the Assyrian conduct against the various groups and nations in the empire.

The words *hin*^{e}*nî 'ēlayik* in 3.5 have the same function as the *Botenformel*, 'thus speaks YHWH', elsewhere in the Hebrew Bible. In 3.5, these words form a bridge with same formula in 2.14. The words announce the forthcoming judgment for the City of Blood. Nineveh will be laid in ruins. The sections end with a degrading rhetorical question on the absence of comforters.

5.1.4.3 Description of the Downfall of Nineveh.

This unit, again, consists in three sub-units:

3.8-13 Comparison with the fate of the Egyptian city 'No Amon'
3.14-17c Summons to strengthen the defensive works
3.17d-19 Concluding questions.

In the first sub-unit, an unnamed city is compared with Thebes in Egypt. Generally, scholars identify this city with Nineveh. This suggestion fits the context and the mention of the king of Assyria in 3.18. The phrase 'Are you better than …' is again a rhetorical question aiming at the forthcoming dismantling of the powers of Assyria. As far as I can see, Jörg Jeremias is the only scholar who argued that Jerusalem has originally been meant, since the powers of Nineveh were too strong in his view (Jeremias 1970: 38-42). With *no' 'āmôn* the city of Thebes in Egypt is referred to (see also Huddelstun 2003; Cook 2017: 137).[2] In Egyptian, the city with the official name *wꜣs.t*, 'scepter (of the Pharaoh)', was also known as *niwt-'imn*, 'the city of Amon'. In the Hebrew Bible, the city is known as *no'* (Jer. 46.25; Ezek. 30.14-16). In the Assyrian inscriptions of Esarhaddon and Ashurbanipal the

2. Vulgate and Targum identify No-Amon with Alexandria, a city in the delta. To these translators the memory of Egyptian Thebes must have faded away and they chose another city that was surrounded by water.

name for Thebes is *ni-'*; the Aramaic indication *n'* occurs in two documents from Elephantine (*TADAE* A4.2:6; A4.4). According to the inscriptions of Ashurbanipal he conquered and devastated the city in 663 BCE:

> [I took the road] in pursuit of Tanutamon (and) I marched as far as the city Thebes, [his] for[tified] city. He saw the assault of my battle array [and] abandoned the city Thebes; he fled to the city K[ip]kipi. With the support of (the god) Aššur and the goddess Ištar, I conquered that city (Thebes) i[n] its [entir]ety. Silver, gold, precious stones, as much [property of] his palace as there was, garment(s) with multi-[colored trim], linen garments, large horses, people—male and female—two tall obelisks [c]ast with shiny zaḫalû-metal, whose weight was 2,500 talents [(and which) stood at] a temple gate, I ripped (them) from where they were ere[ct]ed and [took (them) t]o Assyria. I carried off sub[stanti]al booty, (which was) without number, [from inside the c]ity Thebes. [I made] m[y] weapons [prevail] over [Egypt and K]ush [and (thus) achieved vi]ctory. Wit[h full hand(s), I returne]d [safely] t[o Nineveh, my capital city].
>
> (Ashurbanipal, Prism B RINAP 5,3: iii 37'-57'; Schneider 1988: 68-71; parallel versions in other Prisms only deviate in detail; for a historical context, see Kahn 2006; Renz 2021: 169-70)

This boasting language cannot be confirmed by the archaeological evidence. The archaeological record of Thebes refers to continuity of habitation. The same is true for the written Egyptian evidence. They hint at the fact that after 663 the Egyptian officials were still in office. On the western bank of the Nile near Thebes tombs were built without interruption (Budka 2010; Höflmayer 2021). The 'Dream Stela of Tanutamon' (ed. Eide et al. 1994: 193-209) does not relate a military confrontation with Ashurbanipal nor the conquest of Thebes (see Schneider 1988: 68-71; Seybold 1989: 57-58; Kahn 2006: 265; Fabry 2006: 68-74). This silencing could be based on Egyptian shame about what happened or read as an indication that the conquest never took place. It also implies that the Assyrian writers either mistook the name of the conquered city or constructed a fictional story and spread 'fake news', which is until this day part of war propaganda. Besides, Thebes is never mentioned in the corpus of hundreds of Neo-Assyrian letters (Karlsson 2018: 42). Either way, the Prisms of Ashurbanipal should be seen as vehemently propagandistic, and it should be noted that the author of the book of Nahum knew of this invented tradition.[3]

---

3. This is a historiographical riddle that cannot be solved within the boundaries of this publication.

According to the text in Nahum, No-Amon had a favorable geographic setting (3.8; according to Schneider 1988: 64-68, the imagery would refer to an abundant inundation of the Nile) and various auxiliary troops (3.9). Nevertheless, the city is said to have been conquered (3.10). This undermines the trust so often put in a military defense. Nineveh is compared to the conquered city in Egypt. Nahum's message is clear: when a very well-defended city in Egypt could nevertheless be ruined, then the proud capital of Assyria might have a comparable fate, despite all its defensive works.

There is some irony in the second sub-unit: summons to strengthen the defensive works (3.14-17c). As a result of the comparison, the Assyrians are summoned to improve their defensive works, although the author is aware of the futility of these acts: Nineveh will nonetheless be devastated. There are some correspondences between the two sub-units. The images are sliding over each other. Nahum 3.9 refers to the nations that were like auxiliary forces to Thebes (Cush, Put and Libya). Nahum 3.16-17c refers to Nineveh's auxiliary troops. The numerous merchants, officers and writers, however, are compared to locusts: grazing for their own profit but disappearing at the first sign of danger. In other words, they are untrustworthy and fickle.

The concluding question in the third sub-unit has a comparable composition as the question in 2.12. With Van der Woude, I construe the last word of v. 17 *'ayyām*, 'where?', as the first word of v. 18. The word *nāmû* is not be seen as a verb form but as a noun comparable to Akkadian *nawûm*; *namûn*, 'pasturage; dwelling place' (see Kraus 1976: 172-79) and a synonym to Hebrew *nāweh*. The line then reads: 'Where are the pasturages of your shepherd, king of Assyria, where you nobles used to lie down?' (Van der Woude 1978: 114, 125). The image in this question underscores the forthcoming doom for Nineveh: even the retreat for the nobles will disappear. The motivational part—'Over whom did not come your evil continually?'—connects the downfall of Nineveh with the salvation for the oppressed Levantine states.

5.2 The Conceptual Coherence of the Book of Nahum

The presentation of the contents of the book of Nahum above is an argument for the literary coherence of the text. My display made clear that at the level of language and form the various sub-units interconnect. This view is, however, not the consensus in biblical scholarship on this minor prophet. In the research, three currents are detectable.

1. Scholars who argue for the literary unity of the book of Nahum. Their approach is to search for a meaningful reading assuming that the text is

a unit at the literary level (see, e.g., Van der Woude 1977, 1978; Renaud 1987; Sweeney 1992; Becking 1995; Spronk 1995, 1997; Timmer 2021).
2. Scholars who construe the book of Nahum as a standalone book, being the result of a complex redaction history (e.g. Schulz 1973; Seybold 1989; Jeremias 2019). It should be noted that the assumed layers of redaction differ between the proposals.
3. Scholars who see the book of Nahum as the result of the growth of an original core into the book of the Twelve through various stages of redaction in which the growing book was connected with other texts in the Book of the Twelve (see, e.g., Nogalski 1993a; Wöhrle 2008; Hagedorn 2011). Characteristic for this approach is the fact that the various authors arrive at strongly diverging models although they claim to apply the same methodology.

In the remarks above, I already hinted at the connections between the various elements in the book of Nahum. These connections can be construed as the thread that strings the book together. To this, I would like to add another argument for the unity of the book of Nahum.

The literary-critical and redaction-historical approaches to the book of Nahum are all based on the assumption that there would exist a conceptual discrepancy between the opening hymn (A: 1.2-8) and the rest of the book. This is as such a valid literary-critical or redaction-historical argument. But does such a discrepancy really exist? In my view, this is not present in the book of Nahum. The opening hymn (A: 1.2-8) presents a two-sided image of YHWH as a furious and a consoling deity. The elaboration of this hymn (B: 1.9-14) makes clear that each face of this double-faced deity is directed toward two different groups: a masculine and a feminine group who are not yet identified with existing nations. The third textual element (C: 2.1-3) communicates the idea that the forthcoming salvation will befall Judah, while the rest of the book (D: 2.4–3.19) depicts the fate of Nineveh by the rod of divine wrath. As a result, the book of Nahum can be seen as an expression of provoked divine wrath and its consequences both for the suffering and the provoking side.

5.3 Dating the Book of Nahum

When was this composition written? That is a question that is almost unanswerable. There is no site for dating prophetic texts. Something like www.textinsearchofcontext.org containing a decision tree leading to a perfect match is unfortunately not present. This implies that biblical scholars looking for a context in order to elucidate features in the text they are trying to understand have nothing else at their disposal than the traditional crafts of the guild. I would prefer the 'lock-and-key' method. In my view, a text can be compared to a key. The key-bolt refers to the specifics of a given text: its (main) narrative programme, its use of language and metaphors, its conceptual particulars, and the real-time persons mentioned in the text. This key fits generally more than one hole. I will name two of them. The book of Nahum can be assigned to the Hellenistic period as a reflection of the Maccabaean rebellion against the Seleucid politics. It could also be connected to the end of the Babylonian Exile. In both proposals 'Nineveh' stands as a chiffre for another world power. The book could, however, also productively be connected with the final years of Assyrian hegemony. In my opinion, the oldest hole should be preferred (see also Keller 1972: 407-20; Cathcart 1973b; Rudolph 1975: 143-44; Van der Woude 1977; 1978: 67-76; Deissler 1984: 203; Renaud 1987; Schneider 1988: 72-73; Roberts 1991: 38-39; Sweeney 1992; Spronk 1995, 1997; Johnston 2001a; 2001b: 417; Bosman 2002: 590-91; Petersen 2002: 196-99; Klopper 2003; Lanner 2006: 6-7; Maré and Serfontein 2009; Crouch 2009: 158-73; Cook 2017a; Timmer 2020: 33-34; Wessels 2020: 339; Wenyi 2021: 81-104).

My preference to date the book of Nahum in the Assyrian period is not based only on the references to the conquest of Thebes in 663 BCE and the end of the Neo-Assyrian Empire in 612. A dating between 663 and 612 based solely on these connections with real time would be skating on thin ice since both 'events' could have been implanted as a veil for other 'events' (see Chapman 2004: 103). This implies that I do understand when scholars want to date the book of Nahum—or its various redactions—to a later period (see, e.g., Schulz 1973; Seybold 1989; Nogalski 1993b: 93-128; Fabry 2006; Wöhrle 2008: 24-66; 2018; Hagedorn 2011: 29-90; Baumann 2005; Tuell 2016: 13-14; Jeremias 2018: 11-55; 2019: 9-27; O'Brien 2002: 14-22; 2004: 25-27; Berlejung 2006; Dietrich 2016: 14-19). My problem, however, is twofold: (1) that the redaction-historical operations that give a base to these proposals are far from convincing. Besides, scholars applying the redaction-historical approach arrive at a great variety of results (see also Renz 2021: 43). (2) As Sweeney has shown, a dating of the book of Nahum in the Persian era hardly makes sense (Sweeney 1992: 366-69). Comparable remarks could be made to the view of those scholars who construe the book of Nahum to be a *vaticinium ex eventu* (Schulz 1973: 104-10; Machinist 1997: 181; 2018). I do not see why the words of Nahum, as unspecific as they are to the 'real events', could have been uttered only after 612 BCE.

To substantiate my Assyrian date, however, I would like to refer to a special phenomenon. More than any other book in the Hebrew Bible the book of Nahum is larded both with Assyrianisms and with phrases that should be construed as borrowed from the Assyrian culture of writing.

5.3.1 Significant Assyrianisms

The following Assyrian loanwords can be detected in the book of Nahum (some have been noticed by Cathcart 1973a, 1973b; Van der Woude 1977: 113; Mankowski 2000; and in various commentaries). I do not list words that are merely cognates like Hebrew *bêt* // Assyrian *bît(u)*, 'house'.

	Hebrew		Assyrian	Translation
1.2	*nāṭar* I		*nadāru*	'to rage; be furious'
1.3	*śeʿārā*		*šāru*	'whirlwind'
1.5	*nāśâ*		*nasāsu*	'to sing; wail; complain'
1.12	*šelēmîm*		*šalāmu*	'unharmed; safely'[4]
1.14	*śîm qeber*		*quburi epēšum*	'prepare the tomb'[5]
	kî qallôtā read **kiqallût*		*kiqillutu*	'rubbish dump'[6]
2.1	*bāśar* piel		*basāru* D.	'to bring (good) news'
2.2	**maṣṣārā*		*maṣṣartu*	'lookout-station'
2.3	*geʾôn*		*gaʾûm*	'pride; loftiness'
	bāqaq II		*baqāqu*	'to spread'
2.4	*metullāʿîm*		*tultu*	'red-purple'[7]
2.7	*šaʿarê hannehārôt*		*bab nāri*	'river (sluice) gate'
2.8	**hāʿatallâ*[8]		*etellētu*	'sovereign; queen'
	nāhag		*nagāgu*	'to produce a mournful sound'
3.14	*bôʾ baṭṭîṭ*		*erēbu ṭiṭa*	'to go into the clay'

4. See *CAD* Š, 207-208 (sub 3); Cook 2017a; Renz 2021: 96.
5. See the letter from Mari: ARM 1,8:16-18
6. In a Neo-Assyrian legal transaction one of the commodities is 'a refuse dump (*ki-qil-li-ti*) in front of the gate, belonging to these gentlemen, in Buruqu', SAA 6,31 Rev. 3; see also ADD 37 = SAA 6,200:5; SAA 10,294:15.
7. As extracted from the scale-insect *kermes vermillio*, see *CAD* T, 467; Becker 2021: 11.
8. See Van der Woude 1978: 107.

3.17	minn^{e}zār		maṣṣāru	'guard'
	ṭapsār		ṭupšarru	'writer'
			Sumerian: DUB. SAR	
3.18	nāmû		nāmû	'pasture'9

The transfer of words from one language to another is a perennial phenomenon. The number of examples is dazzlingly high. 'Alcohol' has its origin in Arabic; 'coffee' in Turkish; 'starboard' in Dutch, to mention only a few. Loanwords can be categorized in two categories: importation and substitution (see, e.g., Haugen 1950; Mankowski 2000; Matras 2020). Importation refers to words from another language to identify entities for which no word exists in the receiving language: Akkadian *ekallu* from Sumerian é.gal, 'palace; temple' (see also Hebrew *hêkāl*); English 'potato' from Quechua 'papa'. Substitution refers to the process by which an existing word in the receiving language is replaced with a word from the other language: '*pièce-de-résistance*' substituting for English 'masterwork'. The phenomenon of substitution is sometimes an indication that the speaker wants to identify with the cultural values of the giving language and sometimes a residue of having lived for quite some time among people speaking the other language. Dutch citizens who had lived in what now is Indonesia lard their vocabulary with words of Malayan or Javanese origin: 'rimboe' from the Malayan word *rimbu*, 'wilderness, jungle', is often used as a metaphor for 'chaos'; or 'koeli' from Malayan *kuli*, 'day labourer, who performs heavy physical labour, porter'.

It is remarkable that these Assyrianisms are found throughout the book of Nahum. I read this as an argument for the coherence of the text. Besides, these words place the author of the book of Nahum into an Assyrian context. The author might have lived in an Assyrian-speaking environment or was mimicking the language of those in power.

5.3.2 *Near Eastern Treaty Curses*

In the ancient Near East, powerful kingdoms concluded treaties with the vassal states at their borders, although it might be more appropriate to say that these regulations were imposed on the client kings. With the treaty the vassal pledged obedience toward the greater king and his successor. Greater parts of the texts contain curses that will be executed in case the client king would be disobedient, for instance by stopping the payment of

---

9. See Van der Woude 1978: 125.

the yearly tribute. These so-called treaty curses form a collection of threatening stipulations that are also found in other literary genres from the ancient Near East, such as boundary stones—protecting the border against trespassers—and royal stelae—protecting the depiction of the king against destruction and *damnatio memoriae* (see basically Watanabe 1987; Steymans 1995). In the Hebrew Bible, Deuteronomy 28 contains a series of parallels to these treaty curses (Steymans 1995), while in prophetic texts the forthcoming doom is regularly phrased with curses that are comparable to the Neo-Assyrian and Aramaic treaties (see Hillers 1964; Johnston 2001b; Fabry 2006: 107-108; Cook 2017a; Aster 2018).

In the book of Nahum, the following parallels can be noticed:[10]

    1.4   He bawls against the sea and dries her up,
            and all the rivers he dehydrates
    VTE   May Adad, the canal inspector of heaven and earth, cut off sea[sonal flooding] from your land and deprive your fields of [grain].
            (Succession Treaty of Esarhaddon; VTE § 47; SAA 2, 6:440-41; Johnston 2001b: 430-31; Renz 2021: 72)

Two things are remarkable with this parallel. (1) The echo of this curse is located within the description of a theophany. (2) The succeeding line of the Adad curse (VTE § 47) has an echo in the final line of the opening hymn of the book of Nahum. This gives the impression that the memory on the Adad curse functions as a bracket in the hymn of Nahum holding the parts together.

    1.8   But with an overflowing flood
            he will make a complete end of her place.
    VTE   may he (Adad) [submerge][11] your land with a great flood.
            (Succession Treaty of Esarhaddon; VTE § 47; SAA 2, 6:442; see Spronk 1997: 49; Johnston 2001b: 430-31; 2002: 32-34)

Both the Hebrew Bible and the Assyrian text use a non-standard word for 'flood': *šeṭep* instead of *mabbûl*; *riḥṣu* instead of *abubu*. Both words do not refer to the legendary floods of divine destruction, as in Gilgamesh or the Noah story, but to the military tactic to use water retained behind a dyke to inundate a city and its surroundings.

   10. VTE refers to the Assyrian succession treaty of Esarhaddon; Wiseman 1958; SAA 2, 6; Sefîre refers to the Aramaic treaty between Mattiel, king of Arpad, and Bargayah, king of the enigmatic kingdom KTK; Lemaire and Durand 1984; *KAI* 222.

   11. The text of the recently discovered Tayinat-treaty confirms the suggestion that this verb is implied: *li-ir-ḥi-iṣ*, 'may he submerge' (see Lauinger 2012: T vi,16).

1.8	By pursuing his enemies into darkness
VTE	May Shamash, the light of heaven and earth, not give you a fair and equitable judgment; may he take away your eyesight; may you walk in darkness!
(VTE § 40; SAA 2, 6:422-24; see Johnston 2001b: 423-24)
May your days be dark, your years be dim—may they [the gods] decree dimness without any brightness
(VTE § 56; SAA 2, 6:485-86; see Johnston 2001b: 423-24)
1.14	Your name will no longer be perpetuated.
VTE	May Zarpanitu, who grants name and seed, destroy your name and your seed from the land.
(Succession Treaty of Esarhaddon; VTE § 45; SAA 2, 6:435-36; Chapman 2004: 151)
Sefire	his off[spring] shall have no name
(Sefire I C:24-25; see Jeremias 2019: 106-107; compare Nerab I—*KAI* 225:9-11)

In Nahum, the masculine 'you'-character is threatened with a discontinuation of name and off-spring, a curse that is directed against the trespassers of the loyalty of Esarhaddon (see Johnston 2001b: 424-26; Renz 2021: 99-100).

2.14	The sword shall devour your young lions.
VTE	If you should forsake Esarhaddon, king of Assyria, Assurbanipal, the great crown prince designate, (his brothers, [sons by the same mother] as Assurbanipal, the great crown prince designate, and the other sons, the offspring of [Esa]rhaddon, king of Assyria), going to the south or to the north, may iron swords consume him who goes to the south and may iron swords likewise consume him who goes to the north; may they [slaughter] you, your women, your brothers, your sons, and your daughters like a spring lamb and a kid.
(Succession Treaty of Esarhaddon; VTE § 96-96A; SAA 2, 6:632-636C; see Johnston 2001a: 304-306)

In other words, the threat by which the Assyrian king keeps in line the client kings will be part of the fate of Nineveh. Its 'young lions'—a metaphor for its princes and nobles—will be devoured by the sword. This connection is challenged by Berlejung (2006: 335).

2.14	The voice of your messenger will no longer be heard.
Sefire	Nor may the sound of the lyre be heard in Arpad and among its people.
(Sefire 1 A,29)

This curse has, to my knowledge, no counterpart in the neo-Assyrian texts, but could have been part of the general set of ancient Near Eastern curses.

3.1-3		Woe, city of bloodshed, A complete lie, Filled with plunder— the robbery doesn't stop! The sound of a whip. The sound of the rattling of a wheel, And a rushing horse and a bouncing chariot! A prancing horse, The flash of a sword and a lightning spear, A multitude of pierced piles of corpses, there is no end to the bodies— they stumble over the carrions!
	VTE	([If you should sin against] this [treaty] of Esarhaddon, king of Assyria, [and of] his sons and grandsons,) ditto; just as this chariot is drenched with blood up to its base-board, so may your chariots be drenched with your own blood in the midst of your enemy. (Succession Treaty of Esarhaddon; VTE § 90; SAA 2, 6:612-615; see Spronk 1997: 89)

This a not a clear or full parallel, but the imagery of blood as a result of the charges of inimical chariots is very comparable.

3.5		I will lift your skirts over your face. I will show the nations your nakedness and the kingdoms your shame.
	Sefire	[and just as a pros]ti[tute is stripped naked; So may the wives of Mattiel be stripped naked And the wives of his offspring and the wives of [his] no[bles]. (Sefire 1 A,44; but see the remarks in Jeremias 2019: 174)

To my knowledge, this curse too has no counterpart in the Neo-Assyrian texts, but could have been part of the general set of ancient Near Eastern curses (Renz 2021; 161).

3.7		Nineveh is in ruins who will mourn for her? Where can I find anyone to comfort you?
	VTE	may your ghost have nobody to take care of the pouring of libations to him. (Succession Treaty of Esarhaddon; VTE § 47; SAA 2, 6:452; see Becking 1995; Johnston 2001b: 427; with a comment by Jeremias 2019: 174)

This is not a literary but a conceptual parallel. Both the question 'who will mourn for her?' and the observation 'nobody will take care' refer to an unfinished end of life without the ritual consolation.

> 3.10   Even she (= Thebes) went into exile; into captivity.
> Esarh   May Melqarth and Eshmun deliver your land to destruction and your people to deportation; may they [uproot] you from your land.
>   (Esarhaddon Treaty with Baal of Tyre; SAA 2.5 rev iv:14-15; see Spronk 1997: 131)

This is the only neo-Assyrian text that mentions exile as a curse.

> 3.13   Look, the troops in your midst are like women.
> Ashurnirari   If Mati'-ilu sins against this treaty with Aššur-nerari, king of Assyria, may Mati'-ilu become a prostitute, his soldiers women.
>   (Treaty of Ashurnirari with Mati'el of Arpad; SAA 2, 2 r. v:8-9)

This gender conversion is well known from Mesopotamian texts as an act of Ishtar. See the passage from the Erra epic:

> whose maleness Ishtar turned fe[male] for the awe of the people; carriers of swords, carriers of razors, scalpels, and blades, who break [taboos?] to Ishtar's delight! (Erra Epic IV 56-58)

The same concept is phrased more implicitly in an Old Babylonian hymn:

> May she (= Inanna/Ishtar) change the right side into the left side
> Dress him in the dress of a woman
> Place the speech of a woman in his mouth
> And give him a spindle and a hair-clasp.
>   (UM 29-16-229 ii 4f; see Sjöberg 1975: 224)

In the phrase 'to change the right side into the left side' the words 'right' and 'left' should be construed as euphemisms for 'male' and 'female'. In sum, Nah. 3.13 presents the topos of soldiers losing their manhood and become worthless warriors (see also Lanner 2006: 157-59).

> 3.15   There the fire will consume you;
>   the sword will cut you down—
>   they will devour you like a swarm of locusts.
> VTE   may the locust who diminishes the land devour your harvest
>   (Succession Treaty of Esarhaddon; VTE § 47; SAA 2, 6:442-43 // Treaty of Ashurnirari with Mati'el of Arpad; SAA 2, 2: r. vi 1)
> Sefire   For seven years, may the locust devour (Arpad).
>   (Sefire 1 A,27; see Tawil 1977; Johnston 2001b: 428-29)

The locust has a double meaning. On the one hand, the word refers to an insect that was known for devastating crops before harvest with the result of hunger. On the other hand, the word stands metaphorically for an army flooding an area and extorting its population (see Lanner 2006: 159-60).

> 3.19 There is no relief for your fracture
> Your wound is incurable.
>
> VTE May Anu, king of the gods, let disease, exhaustion, malaria, sleeplessness, worries and ill health rain upon all your houses.
> (Succession Treaty of Esarhaddon; VTE § 38A; SAA 2, 6:418A-C)
> May Gula, the great physician, put sickness and weariness [in your hearts] and an unhealing wound in your body. Bathe in [blood and pus] as if in water!
> (Succession Treaty of Esarhaddon; VTE § 52; SAA 2, 6:461-63)

The trespassing of the treaty would lead to irreversible trauma. It should be noted that this curse is not restricted to vassal treaties or—in the Hebrew Bible—to the context of the covenant. It also appears in sixteen *kudurrus* (boundary stones) and in the texts of various royal stelae (see Watanabe 1987: 35-40; Johnston 2001b: 429-30; Becking 2004: 177-81; Berlejung 2006: 344-45; Jeremias 2019: 210-11). When a line is crossed, the deity will act full of remorse.

In my view, the choice of this kind of images is deliberate in the book of Nahum. The author used elements of the treaty ideology of the Assyrians to depict their own downfall, hence implying that the Assyrians are construed as trespassers by exploiting Judah and Israel (see Becking 1995: 291-93; Johnston 2001b: 21-45; for a different view, see Berlejung 2006).

5.3.3 *Three Idiomatic expressions, a Comparison, and Two Characterizations*

In the book of Nahum two idiomatic expressions occur that have a clear counterpart in Assyrian texts. In Nah. 1.13 the feminine 'you-character' is promised:

> But now, I will break his yoke that is on you
> And your shackles, I will tear apart!

The image is clear: the feminine 'you-character' is compared with a bovine under the harshness that is suffered when ploughing (see Ruwe and Weise 2002). Both in Assyrian inscriptions and in the Hebrew Bible the imagery of the yoke was used to characterize the unequal relationship between a superior and an underlying power: between the Assyrian monarch and a marginal vassal state or between God and Israel (Johnston 2002). The

Hebrew expression 'to break the bond' refers to a change in such a relationship where the lower power shakes off the belittling domination (e.g. Jer. 2.20; 5.5; 30.8-9; Ps. 2.3). An Assyrian counterpart is found in a Neo-Assyrian fragment of the epic of Atrachasis:

...] X *i ni-iš-bi-ir ni-ra*   ...] let us break (his) yoke
(Atr. J; CT 46, 7,2; Lambert and Millard 1969: 14)

From the context it becomes clear that in this fragment the breaking of the yoke refers to an act of liberation of the lower gods—the Igigi—against the ruling sky-gods—the Anunnaki.

In Nah. 2.8 the forthcoming downfall of Nineveh is depicted in a mourning ritual. After the queen is sent naked into exile:

... her handmaids are moaning like the sound of doves,
Beating on their breasts.

In several Mesopotamian texts the expression 'to moan constantly like a dove'—variously phrased—occurs indicating a ritual complaining sound of mourning (e.g. Nergal and Ereshkigal III 7; Ludlul I 107; see Van der Toorn 1985: 190). The presence of both idioms can be seen as an indication that the author of the book of Nahum was familiar with the Neo-Assyrian jargon.

In Nah. 1.8 the fate of God's enemy is described as follows:

But with a rushing flood he will make a complete end of her site.

This line echoes the description of Esarhaddon's victory over Sidon:

I leveled Sidon, his stronghold, which is situated in the midst of the sea, like a flood, tore out its wall(s) and its dwelling(s), (*a-bu-biš as-pu-un* BÀD-*šú*) and threw (them) into the sea.
(Esarhaddon Nineveh A ii:68-70; Leichty 2011: 16; see also Bach 2022: 52-53; see Machinist 1983: 726-27; Christensen 2009: 217; May 2022b: 246-47, for other examples)

Machinist made a note on Nah. 2.11. He compared the line:

bûqâ ûm^e bûqâ ûm^e bullātâ
Desert, desolation, and destruction!

with the Assyrian alliterating phrase:

āla appal aqqur ina išāti ašrup ākulšu
The city I devastated, destroyed, burned with fire, consumed it
(E.g., Aššurnasirpal II in Budge and King 2005: 295:ii 1; 362:iii 54; see Machinist 1983: 724, for a few dozen other instances; Spronk 1997: 102; Christensen 2009: 298)

This is, of course, not a formal parallel, but the presence of the alliteration in both Hebrew and Assyrian might be a strong indication that the author of the book of Nahum was inspired by this way of phrasing.

Finally, I would like to refer to two characterizations. (1) In the opening hymn of the book of Nahum, the God of Israel is characterized as a *noqēm*, 'avenger' (Nah. 1.2-3). On a boundary stone from the reign of Nebuchadnezzar I it is stated:

> *ana turri gi-mil-li Akkadi ušatbâ kakkēšu*
> He (Marduk) made him take up arms in order to avenge Akkad
> (BBSt 6 i:13; twelfth century BCE)

In the Babylonian Creation epic, *Enuma Elish,* Tiamat is summoned by the assembly of the gods to take revenge for the murder of her husband Mummu:

> *gi-mi-la-šu-nu tir-ri*
> Take revenge!
> (EnEl i:122)

This characterization forms an ongoing narrative thread throughout *Enuma Elish* (ii 127; ii 156; iii 10; iii 116, etc). The role of avenger is transferred to Marduk. The theme culminates in the praise of the gods for Marduk (Van de Mierop 2003: 12):

> Of our son, the hero, our avenger (*gi-mil-li-ni*).
> (EnEl vi:163)

In the Zinjirli stele, Esarhaddon receives the epithet:

> *gi-mil a-bi*
> Avenger of (his) father
> (Esarh. Zinj. = Leichty 2011: 184 [Esarhaddon 98]: 25; see Galter 2022: 112).

Not unlike YHWH, the Assyrian gods were characterized as full of revenge, and so were their kings.

(2) In Nah. 3.8 the Egyptian city of No-Amon, which was thought to be unconquerable, is depicted as follows:

> Are you better than Thebes
> that sat by the Nile,
> with water around her,
> her rampart a sea,
> water her wall? (NRSV)

Berger (1970) has hinted at a parallel description in the Annals of Esarhaddon:

The kings who live in the sea, whose (inner) walls are the sea and whose outer walls are the waves, who ride in boats instead of chariots, (and) who harness rowers instead of horses, were seized by fear; their hearts were pounding.

(Esarhaddon Annals Niniveh A, episode 18, IV:82-84; Leichty 2011: 21; Jeremias 2019: 191)

It is unclear which kingdoms are referred to: Phoenician city-states built on islands or peninsulas; cities in the estuary of the Tigris and the Euphrates, or cities in Egypt? In any case it seems as if the author of Nahum is quoting this text or just used an ancient Near Eastern scribal tradition.

5.3.4 *Inversion of the Idiom of Royal Inscriptions*

Angelika Berlejung has scanned the book of Nahum—especially 2.4–3.19—for words and images that can be seen as based on the memory of Assyrian royal inscriptions (Berlejung 2006). She collected many examples. It should be noted that these are not literal representations of Assyrian words and idioms, but allusions to the Assyrian phrasing in their reports of the battles and conquests. She remarkably notes that, quite often, the texts from the book of Nahum can be seen as inversions of Neo-Assyrian *topoi*. Inversion in this context means a reversal of the direction of speech. Where the Assyrian writers used this language to glorify the heroic acts of their kings, the biblical text uses this language to describe the impending fate of the once so mighty power. Timmer classifies this language in the book of Nahum as 'ironic reuse of Assyrian propaganda' (Timmer 2020: 49-50). In a way this use is a form of tit for tat. I will come back to this pattern later (see also Wessels 2014).

5.3.5 *The Language of the Sculptures*

In the palaces of the Neo-Assyrian kings, the walls were decorated with sculptures depicting the conquests of rebellious lands by the king of Assur. They present a 'message produced in the artifact mode' (Wobst 1977). They present the royal gaze on the deeds and doings of the Neo-Assyrian king and hence communicate his power over other kingdoms (Winter 1981). They are not so much impartial pictures of the past, but displays with a message: here you see what will happen to a non-loyal vassal.

Many of these scenes have echoes in the prophecies in the book of Nahum. Various scholars have indicated that this likeliness is not haphazard (Petersen 2002: 197; O'Brien 2002: 17-18; Wenyi 2021: 89-104). In the description of the fate of Nineveh, the prophet makes use of Assyrian imagery, but it is redirected. It is no longer the rebellious kings who will fall prey to these acts, but the Assyrian king himself (Berlejung 2006; Spronk 2018: 241). I will briefly discuss two examples.

Greater parts of the book of Nahum, especially the descriptions of the fall of Nineveh (element D), can be read as voice-over when looking at the wall relief from the southwest palace at Nineveh depicting the siege of the Judaean city of Lachish by King Sennacherib. These reliefs have been edited by Ussishkin (1982) and discussed by Uehlinger (2003). I do not propose a one-on-one match for all scenes. The resemblance of the battle scenes on the reliefs and the phrasing of the texts is, however, remarkably and painfully clear (see Wenyi 2021: 93-104).

A comparable remark can be made about the wall reliefs depicting the battle of Ashurbanipal against Te'uman, the usurper of the throne in Elam. This battle was fought at Til Tuba in 653 BCE. The account on this battle is written in the Annals of Ashurbanipal (e.g. Ashurbanipal Prism B = RINAP 5, 3 v:79-96). The episodes of this battle are carved in the wall reliefs in the southwest palace of Ashurbanipal in Nineveh (Watanabe 2004; Walker 2022: 126-83). The scenes are dramatic and full of violence. Many of the war scenes are echoed in the book of Nahum.

The section Nah. 2.12-14 is full of leonine imagery:

12 Where is the lions' den?
        the pasture of the young lions,
    where the lion went,
        and the lioness
    and the lion's cubs,
        with no one to startle them?
13 Where is the lion who plundered for his whelps
    and throttled for his lionesses?
    He had filled his caves with prey
        and his dens with robbery.
14 'See, I am against you,
        —oracle of Yhwh of hosts—,
    and I will destruct her chariot into smoke,
        and the sword shall devour your young lions;
    I will cut off your prey from the earth,
        and the voice of your messengers shall no longer be heard.'

The wall reliefs of the palace of the Neo-Assyrian king Ashurbanipal contain dozens of scenes in which the king is depicted as an excellent lion-hunter (Albenda 1974; Walker 2022: 184-239). In these images, the lion stands for the 'enemy, everything non-Assyrian' that should be hunted and exterminated (Watanabe 2021; Wenyi 2021: 89-93). The text in Nah.

2.12-14 can be read as an inversion of this pictorial language. The various lions are to be identified with Assyrian citizens, merchants and courtiers. In applying and inverting the boasting self-depiction of the Assyrians in a text that reflects on the impending end of the Assyrian Empire, the counter image functions as a harsh criticism (Wessels 2014).

These observations provide extra arguments for dating the book of Nahum in the period when Assyria was the most important world power. A date after the end of that empire would disarm the words of Nahum.

5.4 Conclusion

The observation that the author of the book of Nahum had a literary knowledge (on this concept see Vanhoozer 2009; Simpson 2013) of Neo-Assyrian at his disposal leads to the conclusion that a Neo-Assyrian context for the book of Nahum—although not indisputably provable—is more than likely. Since this would be the earliest hole in which the key of the text fits, I assume that a dating of Nahum in the Neo-Assyrian era is the most probable possibility.

How did Nahum obtain this literary and pictorial knowledge? On the basis of the presence of various Assyrian loanwords, Van der Woude (1978) construed the book to be a letter written from (Assyrian) exile. To Spronk (1997: 13) this feature was the basis of the following assumption. In his view, Nahum is a pseudonym for a person who functioned as a writer at the court of King Manasseh. In view of the function and the assumed written communication with Assyria, this person had to be able to read and write Assyrian. I would like to bring these assumptions a little bit further with the following—slightly speculative—proposal. Building on an observation by Parpola (2003: 101-102), Sano has argued—with abundant evidence—that the Assyrians recruited talented youngsters from among the exiled elites of the conquered areas in order to educate them and to integrate them into the Assyrian world. Quite often, these educated members of local elites were sent back to the region of origin to defend Assyrian interests in the provinces and the vassal kingdoms (Sano 2020: 63-75). I assume it to be possible that 'Nahum'—whatever his real name and position in the former Judaean elite were—had been educated in this way and returned to Jerusalem to act as an Assyrian middle-man. When confronted with the traumatic reality in the vassal kingdom of Judah and the province of Samerina, he found the need to write a subversive pamphlet.

As for the imagery, I imagine that Nahum during his education at the court of Assyria most certainly had seen these impressive sculptures. The readership of the book of Nahum lived with the traumatic memory of events such as the gruesome conquest of Lachish.

Although the Hebrew Bible presents hardly any bibliography of Nahum (except of his birthplace, the enigmatic El Qosh; see Christensen 2009: 57), I would nevertheless formulate a proposal. Above (3.2.2), I have referred to the evidence indicating that selected deportees had been educated by the Assyrians in 'Assyrian literature, science and the ways of life in general' resulting in literary knowledge of Neo-Assyrian texts and idioms. In combination with the manifold parallels with the Assyrian literature in the book of Nahum, I dare to formulate the assumption that the author of this biblical book has been one of those selected deportees. Later, when employed in Israel or Judah, he turned against his masters. This constructed biography has parallels in the age of Western colonialism. Students from the former Dutch colony now known as Indonesia who returned to their homeland after an education in the Netherlands became more and more aware of the local misery that colonialism had brought. They became the kernel of the Merdeka, or strive for independence, movement (Adam 1995; Van Reybrouck 2020).

6

Trauma for a Trauma:
The Fate of Assyria and its Problems

6.1 Introduction

In the previous chapters, I have argued for two views on the past:

- The inhabitants of the Assyrian province Samerina, as well as those who lived in the client kingdom of Judah, suffered from the presence of the Assyrians. The yoke on them had various elements: loss of independence, deportations, paying of tribute, etc. This suffering was perceived as trauma.
- The book of Nahum was written during this period of Assyrian rule, probably in the final decades of it by a person who had inside knowledge of Assyrian culture and language.

The question I now would like to discuss is the following: in what way is the book of Nahum to be seen as a consoling reaction to this trauma? In order to answer this question, three topics need to be discussed.

1. Which consolation is promised to Judah and Israel?
2. What fate awaits Nineveh?
3. What reason is given for all this?

I will discuss these three topics in the next sections.

6.2 Which Consolation Is Promised to Judah and Israel?

The future for Israel and Judah is depicted in element C (2.1-3). I would translate these lines as follows:

2.1	Intr	See on the mountains
		the feet of the messenger
		announcing peace.
	Imp	Celebrate, Judah, your feasts!
		Pay your vows!
	Mot	Because it will no longer happen
		that the Wicked One (Belial) will pass through you.
		He is eliminated completely!
2.2	Intr	The scattered one will come up to you.
	Imp	Look out from your lookout-station!
		Keep watch over the road!
		Strengthen the loins!
		Make firm with abundant power!
2.3	Mot	Because YHWH returns
		with the pride of Jacob, which is the pride of Israel,
		Since destroyers have destroyed them
		and their protectors are devastated.

As noted above, this short unit is composed in two sets with a comparable structure: Van der Woude (1978: 116) labelled them: introduction—summons—motivation of the summons. This composition presents a strong argument against the view that Nah. 2.1 (ET 1.15) should be seen as the closing line of the opening chapter (thus Roberts 1991: 42-55) as well as for the view that the unit is to be seen as the result of a redaction-historical process and was originally addressed against Judah (Jeremias 1970: 25-28). Below, I will argue for a different label of the first element. First, a few remarks on text and translation.

2.1 *mᵉbaśśēr* Piel participle of the verb *bśr*, 'to bring a message, news'. This news is not by definition 'positive' or 'good' for the receiver. It is the amplifier 'announcing peace' that stipulates the character of the message (see Chapman 2004: 100).

2.2 *mēpîṣ* A noun derived from the verb *pûṣ* hiphil, 'to scatter', meaning 'the scattered' (the hiphil of this verb can have intransitive force; Van der Woude 1978: 116-17) and not the 'scatterer' (e.g. Jeremias 1970: 26; Schulz 1973: 26; Rudolph 1975: 158; Renaud 1987: 294; Roberts 1991: 55; Spronk 1997: 59; O'Brien 2002: 59; Pinker 2003b, who assumes the word refers to the cavalry attacking Nineveh; O'Brien 2004: 41; Lanner 2006: 82, 93-94, 121-22; Fabry 2006: 158-60; Wöhrle 2008: 26-28; Christensen 2009: 262-63; Hagedorn 2011: 33; Dietrich 2016: 57; Tuell 2016: 34; Jeremias 2019: 120; Timmer 2020: 120; Renz 2021: 111-12). This reading also implies that the address of 2.2 is Judah and not Nineveh.

mṣrh This noun should be read **maṣṣārā*, 'lookout-station'; cf. Assyrian *maṣṣartu*, 'watch-house' (*CAD* M1: 336-37).

2.3 *šāb* This word has been treated differently. Some scholars construe it as a form of the verb *šbb*, 'to cut off' (e.g. Maier 1959: 233; Jeremias 1970: 27; 2019: 120). This proposal does not make much sense in the context; besides it is not supported by the ancient versions. Others plead for a form of the verb *šûb*, 'to restore' (e.g. *DCH* 8, 288-98; Rudolph 1975: 158; Roberts 1991: 55; Nogalski 1993b: 113-14; Spronk 1997: 86-87; O'Brien 2002: 59; Lanner 2006: 82, 94; Wöhrle 2008: 26; Crouch 2009: 166-67; Christensen 2009: 265; Hagedorn 2011: 33; Dietrich 2016: 42; Tuell 2016: 35; Timmer 2020: 124; Renz 2021: 111-12; Wenyi 2021: 116). Fabry chose for the meaning 'zurückweisen (to refuse, reject)' (Fabry 2006: 158). The verb *šûb* in the qal, however, is intransitive and should be rendered with 'to return' (Van der Woude 1977: 117; 1978: 97-98; Renaud 1987: 296; *DCH* 8, 273-88). This implies that the particle *'et* is not the *nota objecti*, but should be construed as the preposition 'with'.

gᵉ'ôn 'Pride', not 'hubris, haughtiness' (contra e.g. Keller 1972: 401), or 'majesty' (Crouch 2009: 166-67).

zᵉmorêhem This masculine noun cannot be the plural of the feminine noun *zᵉmôrā*, 'vine', or 'branch' (Jeremias 1970: 26; Lanner 2006: 82, 125-27; Timmer 2020: 124), but should be construed as a noun derived from the verb *III zmr // šmr*, 'to guard'; cf. Ugaritic *ḏmr*, 'to guard' (Cathcart 1973a: 85-86; Van der Woude 1978: 118-19, 'soldier'). I propose to render with 'protectors', a word vaguely referring to the spirits of the ancestors.

Introduction or oracle? Van der Woude labelled the first element as 'introductory clause' (1977: 116; 1978: 97-98). In my view, this is a rather vague classification. Both 'introductions' present an image of one or more persons on their way to an unnamed city, most probably Jerusalem. Both the 'bringer of good tidings' and the 'scattered one' are on their way to a better future. In my view, this hints at a classification as an oracle of salvation.

Judah is summoned in two slightly different dimensions. They are called to celebrate their festivals and to pay their vows. Which festivals and what kind of vows are not elaborated. I will come to that later. The second summons is more of a military character. Judah should be prepared for the worst and be able to protect and guide the homecomers on their last trajectory to Jerusalem.

The summons are also motivated in two dimensions. On the one hand, 'the wicked one' will no longer set his devastating feet on Judaean soil, since he will be eliminated. The author applies here the adverbial device for discontinuity *lo'* ... *'ôd*, 'no ... longer' (see Becking 2004: 235-37). The trauma bringing Belial will soon find its end. On the other hand, those deported from the area of Samaria will return with YHWH from their exile. They are characterized as the 'pride of Jacob'.

From the point of view of trauma studies, a few remarks can now be made. The author of this unit accepts the trauma inflicted on Israel by exile. The label 'the scattered one' refers to the misery of deportation all over the Assyrian Empire. The Hebrew verb used here, *pûṣ*, occurs some sixty times in the Hebrew Bible and indicates the dispersal to all four corners of the earth, away from the homeland. This dispersal is seen as a heavy burden on the Israelites, who are soon to be redeemed. Nahum 2.1-3 does not contain a reference to guilt. There is no (self-)blame for the risen situation. Blaming oneself for an inflicted trauma is—too often—a traumatic reaction (see e.g. Blaxter 1993; Unthank 2019; Jacobsen and Petersen 2022). The author of this textual unit accepts the trauma of Judah and Israel that was imposed by *bᵉliyya'al*, 'the Wicked One'—a nickname for any Assyrian king (Chapman 2004: 153) or any other oppressor, for instance, Antiochus IV Epiphanes *until this day* (Jeremias 2019: 113-16). This word *bᵉliyya'al*, 'the Wicked One', was already mentioned in Nah. 1.11: 'From you shall depart one who plots evil against the Yʜᴡʜ, one who counsels wickedness (*bᵉliyya'al*)'. The suffix in *mimmēk*, 'from you', is feminine. The verb *yāṣa'*, 'to take off, depart', evokes the image that 'the Wicked One' will no longer set his devastating feet on the soil of the 'feminine-you'. The language in 1.11 and 2.1 makes clear that Judah had suffered from this 'Wicked One', which can be seen as a depreciating mockery for the Assyrian yoke.

In the first summons, Judah is called to:

> Celebrate, Judah, your feasts!
>   Pay your vows! (2.1)

It is uncertain which festivals are to be celebrated, but one can guess that festivities by which Yʜᴡʜ is thanked for ending the period of trauma are implied (Christensen 2009: 260). Two moments in the narrative Ezra 3–6 can be given as parallels. After the return from exile, the returnees gathered in Jerusalem to bring burnt offerings and to celebrate the festival of Booths (Ezra 3.1-6). In Ezra 6.16, it is narrated that 'The children of Israel, the priests, and the Levites, and the rest of the children of the captivity, celebrated the dedication of this house of God with joy'. In view of the parallelism, the festivals mentioned here could also have been rituals in payment of vows. Up to our times, the end of a traumatic period is welcomed by communal joy, whether or not channeled into official festivities. The *Wende* as a result of the tearing down of the Berlin Wall is a case in point.

Vows are characteristic of those in need. That is a fact of all times and all places. Uttering a vow is often a step in the mourning process. In a cry for help out of despair, humans make promises that sometimes are too great to be fulfilled. See for instance Mic. 6.6-7. In the book of Deuteronomy, the seriousness of a vow is indicated:

> If you make a vow to the LORD your God, do not postpone fulfilling it; for the LORD your God will surely require it of you, and you would incur guilt. But if you refrain from vowing, you will not incur guilt. Whatever your lips utter you must diligently perform, just as you have freely vowed to the LORD your God with your own mouth. (Deut. 23.21-23 NRSV).

When covered in trauma, persons are making vows hoping for an end of the dire situation. The theme 'vow' in the context of the book of Nahum is an indirect indication of the mourning the Assyrian yoke brought over the people in Israel and Judah (see, e.g., Cartledge 1992; Berlinerblau 1996; Christensen 2009: 260; Gudme 2013; Renz 2021: 103-104).

There are two ways to look at the expression g^e'$ôn$ $ya^{'a}qob$, 'the pride of Jacob'. (1) The words can be construed as a reference to the exiled inhabitants of the former Northern Kingdom. They will return guided by their God. The words then refer to a transformation. Having been in trauma, low and scattered, the Israelites will be liberated into a position of loftiness and pride. (2) The expression could refer to a divine being. This interpretation is based on texts such as Hos. 5.5; 7.10 and Amos 6.8. In these texts, the noun g^e'$ôn$ could easily be seen as an indication of a divine being. This interpretation would tally with the fact that the Assyrians (and later the Babylonians) had the habit of returning back divine images to territories that were no longer threatening to their power (see Becking 2006). Problematic with this second interpretation, however, is the fact that in the books of Hosea and Amos, the noun g^e'$ôn$ clearly refers to a god other than YHWH. It would be strange when such an 'other god' would return from exile. In sum, the expression refers to the return from exile of a people that will no longer be in the trauma of humiliation.

In sum, the consolation promised to Israel and Judah consists of two elements: (1) return to the land and (2) the disappearance of the oppressing enemy. In this new future the trauma can be healed.

6.3 What Fate Awaits Nineveh?

The forthcoming doom for Assyria is outlined in the three parts of the textual element D of the book of Nahum (2.4–3.19).

6.3.1 Description of the Assault on Nineveh

In the description of the downfall of Nineveh, the author of the book of Nahum proves his literary geniality. He phrases his message in short staccato-like sentences. These are all short fragments that alternate quickly.

The text resembles an assembled and edited movie. Each new image is seen from a new perspective. All this evokes a realistic and lively depiction of the forthcoming fate of Nineveh. Basic to the description of Nineveh is the underlying concept of the city as a body, that could be attacked like a rapist attacks a woman (2.4-14), that could act like a ravishing harlot (3.1-7), and as a mother (3.10), as Karolien Vermeulen has argued (2017). I disagree with the view of Seybold (1989) that these descriptions go back to the songs of boasting soldiers.

Aside, the final fall of Nineveh by the hands of the Babylonians—with some help by the Medes—is narrated in a Babylonian Chronicle written in 500 BCE:

> The fourteenth year: The king of Akkad mustered his army and marched to Assyria. The king of the Medes marched towards the king of Akkad and they met one another at (...)-u. The king of Akkad and his army crossed the Tigris; Cyaxares had to cross the Radanu, and they marched along the bank of the Tigris. In the month Simanu, the (...)th day, they encamped against Nineveh.
>
> From the month Simanu until the month Âbu—for three months—they subjected the city to a heavy siege. On the Ninth day of the month Âbu they inflicted a major defeat upon a great people. At that time Sin-šar-iškun, king of Assyria, died. They carried off the vast booty of the city and the temple and turned the city into a ruin heap. The (...) of Assyria escaped from the enemy and, to save his life, seized the feet of the king of Akkad.
>
> On the twentieth day of the month Ulûlu, Cyaxares and his army went home. After he had gone, the king of Akkad dispatched his army and they marched to Naṣibina. Plunder and exiles (...) and they brought the people of Rusapu to the king of Akkad at Nineveh. On the (...) of the month (...) Aššur-uballiṭ ascended to the throne in Harran to rule Assyria. Up until the (...) day of the month (...) the king of Akkad set out and in (...).
>
> (Babylonian Chronicle 3:38-52; BM 21901; see Grayson 1975, 94-95; Timmer 2021: 164-65)

In a report written many ages after the event, Diodorus Siculus narrates a fragment from Ctesias that describes the fate of Nineveh:

> Now there was a prophecy which had come down to him from his ancestors: 'No enemy will ever take Ninus by storm unless the river shall first become the city's enemy'. Assuming, therefore, that this would never be, he held out in hope, his thought being to endure the siege and await the troops which would be sent from his subjects. The rebels, elated at their successes, pressed the siege, but because of the strength of the walls they were unable to do any harm to the

men in the city; for neither engines for throwing stones, nor shelters for sappers, nor battering-rams devised to overthrow walls had as yet been invented at that time. Moreover, the inhabitants of the city had a great abundance of all provisions, since the king had taken thought on that score. Consequently the siege dragged on, and for two years they pressed their attack, making assaults on the walls and preventing inhabitants of the city from going out into the country; but in the third year, after there had been heavy and continuous rains, it came to pass that the Euphrates, running very full, both inundated a portion of the city and broke down the walls for a distance of twenty stades.

(Ctesias apud Diodorus Siculus, *Works* II 26:9–27:1)

This description should be seen as legendary, without much historical value. By the time of the Neo-Assyrian Empire, for instance, 'engines for throwing stones' and 'battering rams' had been invented and used in warfare (see MacGinnis 1988; Pinker 2006; Crouch 2015; Wenyi 2021: 83-84; May 2022b: 243-45; Christensen 2009: 284; Renz 2021: 129-30).

Some themes and motives occur both in the Babylonian Chronicle and in Nah. 2.4-14. This should not lead to the conclusion that one text is quoting the other. The book of Nahum was not written after the downfall of Nineveh using the phraseology of the Babylonian Chronicle. Nor did the author of this chronicle use the text of Nahum to compose his description. These themes and phrases occur in many Assyrian and Babylonian inscriptions describing the sack of a city. In my view, the resemblances indicate that the author of the book of Nahum was well versed in the phraseology of the description of a devastation used by the Assyrian scribes.

6.3.2 Threatening Words against Nineveh

The Hebrew text of Nah. 2.4-14 can be rendered as follows:

4 The shields of his warriors have become red;
    his courageous men are clothed in scarlet.
  In the firelight of steel stand the chariots
    on the day of the roll call;
  the spear shafts are brandished.
5 The chariot races madly through the streets;
    they run past themselves on the plaza;
  their appearance is like torches;
    like lightning bolts they dash back and forth.
6 He remembers his majestic ones;
    they stumble in their going;
  they hasten to her wall,
    and the mantelet is set up.

7   The gates of the streams open up;
        the palace melts away.
8   A wagon takes the queen into exile,
        her slave girls moan,
    while as with a pigeon's voice.
        they beat their breasts.
9   Nineveh was like a pond, full of waters
        during the days of her existence.
    Yet they stream away. 'Stand still, stand still!'
        but there is no one who returns.
10 'Plunder the silver;
        plunder the gold!
    Since there is no end to the stock,
        an abundance of all things desirable!'
11 Desert, desolation and destruction!
        A fainting heart and trembling knees.
    And anguish in all loins;
        all their faces gather darkness!
12 Where is the lions' den?
        the pasture of the young lions,
    where the lion went,
        and the lioness
    and the lion's cubs,
        with no one to startle them?
13 Where is the lion who plundered for his whelps
        and throttled for his lionesses?
    He had filled his caves with prey
        and his dens with robbery.
14 'See, I am against you',
        —oracle of Yhwh of hosts—,
    'and I will destruct her chariot into smoke,
        and the sword shall devour your young lions;
    I will cut off your prey from the earth,
        and the voice of your messengers shall no longer be heard'.

This literary unit consists of eight scenes and is closed by an ironical question (2.13-14). The unit reads like a script for a movie with quickly changing scenes (Renaud 1987: 298-99; Premstaller 2003). I will now scan them for trauma-related issues.

- *Roll call* (2.4). The scene describes the gathering and the preparation of the warriors of the assaulting army. Their shields and spears are painted scarlet as a deterrent gesture. These colors anticipate the forthcoming victory and the blood of the vanquished. At the military camp, the

brushed-up chariots glitter in the sunlight. These images describe the materialization of the divine wrath against Nineveh and are the starting point for the end of the traumatic situation.
- *Advance* (2.5). The army starts to move and tears over the roads. The nocturnal advance is a terrifying expression of the divine rage against Nineveh.
- *Siege* (2.6). No sooner have they reached the city than the next battle takes place. There is no time for a bar of rest in this war song. 'The majestic ones' refer to the elite troops who specialized in the siege of walled cities. Assyrian reliefs have captured evocative memories of this type of siege (see, e.g., Ussishkin 1982; with Wenyi 2021). In this image, the author of Nahum turns the picture around: now the Assyrians are the besieged. They are no longer able to wreak trauma, but will themselves be traumatized.
- *A hole elsewhere* (2.7). As the attack continues on the landward side of the city, a breach is made along the Tigris River. These water gates were heavily defended and difficult to capture. See for instance the remark in the Annals of Sennacherib: 'A canal-gate [I built]' (Sennacherib Bavian Inscription:30; see Fabry 2006: 172-74; Christensen 2009: 283). Nevertheless, the besiegers manage to penetrate the city. How, is unknown. This must have been traumatic for proud Nineveh. Before stranding in all-too-realistic notions, it should be noted that the 'streams' here should be seen as also having a mythic connotation. The word *nahrôt* contains a wink to the primordial streams and their devastating powers (Keller 1972: 410-11; Schulz 1973: 66-67; Crouch 2009: 164). The verb *nāmôg* takes up a theme from the hymn in Nah. 1.2-8. The epiphany of God results in: 'Mountains tremble for him, and the hills melt away (*hitmogāgû*)' (1.5; see also Wenyi 2021: 163). The 'melting away' of the palace in 2.7 makes concrete the mythic language into the reality of the impending end of Nineveh. I here adopt the criticism of Wenyi (2021: 85) of the view of Machinist that the verb *mûg* in Nahum would refer to the flooding of the city (Machinist 1997: 191); Machinist seems to be driven by the wish to concur Nahum with the legendary description of the fall of Nineveh by Ctesias.
- *Exile* (2.8). The Hebrew text of v. 8 is not easily understood. Many proposals have been made. I adopt the view of Adam van der Woude (1978, 106-107), who proposed to read *haṣṣab*, 'a wagon", instead of the incomprehensible *huṣṣab* (some interpreted this word as the name of an otherwise unknown queen Hutsab: Ibn Ezra; Kimchi; Dutch Liesvelt Bijbel (1526); KJV; Dutch Staten Vertaling (1637); Beibl William Morgan (Welsh); or as a form of the verb *nāṣab*, 'to stand': Roberts 1991: 55; Lanner 2006: 95, 129-33; Christensen 2009: 287-88; Hagedorn 2011: 34; Tuell 2016:

36; Jeremias 2019: 122; Renz 2021: 115). The reading by van der Woude is supported by the Greek text in the Minor Prophets Scroll from Nahal Hever as well as by the Targum. Next to that Van der Woude restored *hoʿlātâ*, 'she will be brought up", into *hāʿtallâ*, 'sovereign, queen' (Van der Woude 1978: 106-107; cf. Assyrian *etellētu*, 'queen, ruler'; Rudolph 1975: 166, 'Hochedle'; Renaud 1987: 300, *'princesse'*; Roberts 1991: 55, 'princess'; Hagedorn 2011: 34 *'Hochedle'*). Since the Assyrian noun could refer to a queen as well as to a goddess (*CAD* E, 381-83) it might be possible that Nah. 2.8 indicates the exile of an Assyrian goddess whose image is carried away on a wagon. Aron Pinker offered an even more bewildering proposal, following a suggestion made by Delcor that *ḥuṣṣab* should be construed as an allusion to Ishtar (1977; see Spieckermann 1982: 219). In his view, *ḥuṣṣab* refers to a statue of Ishtar. He construes *gulleṯâ* as meaning 'she was denuded, she was exiled'. The word *hoʿlātâ* is read by him as Allatu and seen as a reference to the deity Ereshkigal. All this leads to the conclusion that Nah. 2.8 would contain a reference to the Mesopotamian myth of Ishtar's descent—or exile—to the netherworld (Pinker 2005; see also Timmer 2020: 132-34). Spronk bestows a very specific meaning to the word *hoʿlātâ*. He, correctly, construes the form as a hophal. He then refers to Gen. 31.10, where the qal of the verb *ʿlh* is used as an euphemism for 'to mate', and jumps to the conclusion that the queen received a beastly treatment by the inimical soldiers and translates 'she is raped' (Spronk 1995: 173; 1997: 98; adopted by Wenyi 2021: 164, 177). There are too many unverifiable assumptions in Spronk's argument to accept his view. Either way, the line indicates that the power structure at Nineveh collapses (Jeremias 2019: 141-42). The forthcoming downfall of Nineveh is depicted in a mourning ritual performed by her handmaids, who are moaning like doves and beating on their breasts. I am not convinced by the proposal of Renaud (1987: 302) that these 'handmaids' were prostitutes connected to the cult. As already mentioned above (6.3.3), in several Mesopotamian texts the expression 'to moan constantly like a dove'—variously phrased—occurs, indicating a ritual complaining sound of mourning (e.g. Nergal and Ereshkigal III 7; Ludlul I 107; see Van der Toorn 1985: 190; Christensen 2009: 292; Jeremias 2019: 142). The trauma inflicted by the Assyrians will return to them like a boomerang.

- *No hold* (2.9). The author takes up the geographical location of Nineveh on the Tigris. The city was like a pond full of water, but not anymore. The image of the water is symbolic of the abundant wealth of the city. But everything will disappear and evaporate. Berlejung refers in this connection to the fact that since the reign of Sennacherib, Nineveh was 'the water city' as a result of the building activities of this king (Berlejung 2006: 220-31), for instance the well-known Jerwan aquaduct (most recently Fales 2022).

- *Spoliation* (2.10). The perspective is reversed to the penetrating besiegers. They are summoned to plunder the treasures of the city. The word 'desirable' has two sides. On the one hand, the adjective refers to all the prey stolen by the Assyrians; on the other hand, the word indicates the spoils of war that will become private income for the besiegers. At the background stands the concept of the *ius talionis*, the reciprocal justice of measure for measure (see Crüsemann 1987; Otto 1994: 73-81; Bosman 2002: 597; Van de Mierop 2003; O'Brien 2004: 50; Garber 2008: 290; Crouch 2009: 169-72; Jacobs 2021).
- *Debris and disorder* (2.11). The author offers a final view of the devastated city. The words stumble against one other. The verse is a nice example of homoioteleuton, the repetition of endings in words (Noegel 2021: 250). The chaos of the reality is caught in a semantic staccato. The staccato sentences should be seen as the expression of a traumatic experience. This reality is well known to us through the reports and images from the battlefields of our time (Ukraine, Palestine/Israel for instance; see also Wenyi 2021). These reports are written in a shaken-up language, applying the grammar of astonishment and fear (see Berlejung 2006: 331-33). The once proud city will be humiliated and traumatized.

After these eight scenes, which give a window into the forthcoming traumatic downfall of Nineveh, the section is closed by an ironic question (2.12-13) and a threatening speech (2.14). The ironic question consists in two lines that both have the character of a rhetorical question. The author looks beyond the day of Nineveh's downfall and asks, 'Where is the powerful Nineveh?' The answer can only be: 'Gone! Disappeared! Devastated!' As in a funeral oration, the author boasts the great and important acts of Nineveh, but in an ironic way, indicating that the Assyrian deeds and doings had a shadowy side. Assyria is depicted as a lion robbing for its children, that is, the court and all its servants, but assumes that this looting had a negative impact on the inhabitants of the provinces and the client kingdoms. The yearly tribute implied that the peripheral economies were skimmed in favor of the core area of Assyria. As a response to this trauma, the lion will soon find his end (Schulz 1973: 31-32).

The leonine imagery is quite adequate as a depiction of the Neo-Assyrian rulers (Johnston 2001a; Bosman 2002: 593; O'Brien 2002: 62; Watanabe 2002: 42-56; 2021; Chapman 2004, 73; Lanner 2006: 136-39; Strawn 2005: 46-65; Berlejung 2006: 333-35; Christensen 2009: 323-25; Wessels 2014; Clines 2015; Snyman 2020; Timmer 2020: 141-42; Renz 2021: 141-46; Wenyi 2021: 89-93). Various Assyrian reliefs present kings like Ashurbanipal as lion-hunters (Cornelius 1989; Watanabe 2021: 115-18; Renz 2021:

146; Walker 2022: 184-239). The image is also present in royal inscriptions: Esarhaddon is supposed to have said, *lab-biš an-na-dir-ma*, 'I raged like a lion' (Esarhaddon Nin. A i:53-62; Leichty 2011: 13 // Esarhaddon Prism D i' i':1'-9'; Leichty 2011, 47, and elsewhere; see Watanabe 2021: 113). Some Assyrian kings boasted that they were 'a virile lion' (*lab-ba-ku*) (Watanabe 2021: 113-14). Paradigmatic is a text from Ashurbanipal:

> I, Ashurbanipal, king of the world, king of Assyria, while enjoying myself on foot, seized a fierce lion that was born in the steppe (UR.MAḪ [*nēšu*]) by its ear and, with the support of (the god) Aššur and the goddess Ishtar—the lady of battle—pierced its body with the lance that was in my hand.
> (Ashurbanipal, fragment of a wall slab that once lined one of the walls of Room S¹ = RINAP 5/2, 56:1-3)

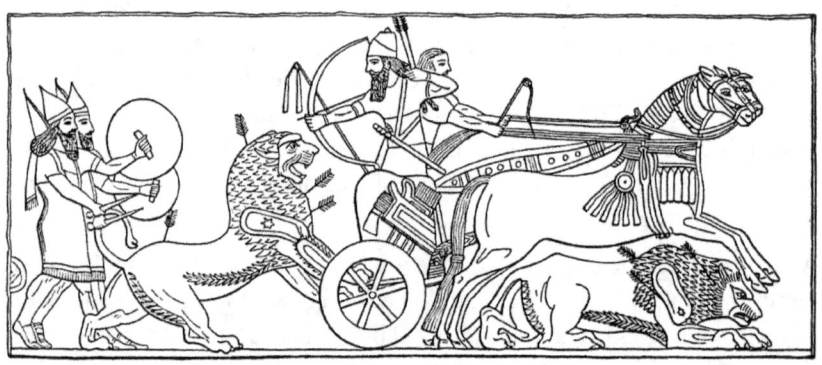

FIGURE 3: The Assyrian king Ashurbanipal as lion-hunter
https://commons.wikimedia.org/wiki/File:Assyrian_king_hunting_lions.png

Nahum 2.12-14 should be read as a form of 'resistance literature'. In the Assyrian texts and images, the lion stands for the 'enemy, everything non-Assyrian' that should be hunted and exterminated (Wenyi 2021: 89-93). The author of Nahum turns this language upside down by identifying the various lions with Assyrian citizens, merchants and courtiers. In applying and inverting the boasting self-depiction of the Assyrians in a text that reflects on the impending end of the Assyrian Empire, the counterimage functions as a harsh criticism (Wessels 2014).

The section is concluded by a threatening speech in which Nineveh is ridiculed (2.14; Wessels 2020: 342).[1] This phrase, 'See I am against you!',

---

1. On text-critical problems in this verse and especially the presence of feminine suffixes next to masculine ones, see Hartog 2013.

is attested in Nahum (twice), Jeremiah (four times), and Ezekiel (fourteen times). The author of the book of Nahum presents this threat as a divine speech. Part of the threat is the 'destruction of her chariot into smoke'. Traditionally, the form *hib'artî* is construed as a hiphil from the verb *b'r*, 'to burn'. This rendition presents a problem of understanding the image: a chariot can be burned by fire, not by smoke (see Pinker 2004). I would propose that the word is a form of the verb *b'r* II, 'to destroy, clear away' and that the preposition *b* has final force here. This would avoid an emendation such as the one proposed by Pinker: *his'artî*, 'I will twirl' (Pinker 2004).

There is more at stake than a political-military conflict: YHWH will liberate his people from the trauma inflicted (Wessels 2020: 342-43). The final clause stands in contrast to the first line of ch. 2. Over against the messengers bringing tidings of comfort and joy stands the cold promise that the voice of the Assyrian envoys will no longer be heard (for a parallel with the Aramaic Sefire treaty 1 A,29, see above, 5.3.2).

6.3.3 Woe-Oracle and a Word of Judgment (3.1-7)

The next section is molded in the literary form of a woe-oracle. This term refers to a literary genre in which a person or a group is bewailed before any evil has happened to them. The genre elaborates on the mourning cry with which a person is mourned after that person's death. In applying this form to the living, an author classifies the life of a person or a group as having reached a dead end: a mourning cry will be their inevitable fate (Westermann 1964, 137-42; Janzen 1972). The majority of scholars—correctly—construe this unit as a threatening description of the forthcoming end of Nineveh (e.g. Timmer 2020: 147-58; Wessels 2020: 344-46). Jeremias is of the opinion that the words are directed against Jerusalem (1970: 28-37). The imaginary used in 3.1-7—the city as a harlot—does not fit as a description of Jerusalem as intended target. I translate these lines as follows:

1 Woe, city of bloodshed,
    A complete lie,
  Filled with plunder—
    the robbery doesn't stop!
2 The sound of a whip.
    The sound of the rattling of a wheel,
  And a rushing horse
    and a bouncing chariot!
3 A prancing horse,
    The flash of a sword
      and a lightning spear,

>   A multitude of pierced
>   piles of corpses,
>   there is no end to the bodies—
>   they stumble over the carrion!
>
> 4   Because of the countless prostitutions of the prostitute,
>   excellent in grace,
>   a mistress of enchantment,
>   who sells nations through her prostitution
>   and clans through her sorcery,
>
> 5   'See, I am against you,'
>   —oracle of Y<small>HWH</small> of hosts—,
>   'I will uncover your skirts up to your face,
>   I will show the nations your nakedness
>   And kingdoms your dishonor.
> 6   I will throw filth at you,
>   I will taunt you,
>   I will put you to watch,
> 7   so that whoever sees you
>   will flee from you
>   and say:
>   "Nineveh is devastated;
>   who will mourn for her?"
>   Where shall I seek comforters for you?'

This unit has a concentric structure:

- A   Woe oracle
- B   Motivation
- C   Prophecy of doom

Important for my interpretation is the fact that I construe the preposition *min* in v. 4 as having a causal force and hence make v. 4 as the motivation for the doom proclaimed in the surrounding units.

Verses 1-3 are molded as a woe-oracle. This textual form traditionally consists of three elements: address, accusation and announcement.

- The address is Nineveh, named as a city of blood (3.1a; contra Jeremias 1970: 28-31, who argues for an identification with Jerusalem; see the criticism of this view in Keller 1972; in his commentary Jeremias 2019: 159 denounced this view). The source of the blood is not mentioned by the author. This invites the reader to think about it. Is it war-accompanying blood? Or does the image refer to Nineveh as a menstruating woman (Claassens 2021)?

- The accusation is found in 3.1b-d: the deeds and doings of the world power are classified as a pack of lies resulting in robbery. These words summarize the trauma inflicted on the provinces and the vassal states and evaluate them as bloody greed.
- The announcement consists of a rephrasing of the impending attack on the city as already presented in 2.4-11 (O'Brien 2002: 66-67). The clauses in 3.2-3 continue the staccato-character of the previous unit. In a handful of flashing images the disaster is described. People will die as a result of the violence (O'Brien 2002: 67). This implies that I do not construe 3.2-3 as a description of the military acts of Nineveh (contra e.g. Van der Woude 1978: 110). They are not part of the accusation.

In the axis of the unit (3.4) Nineveh is depicted in two evaluative images: a harlot and a sorceress (O'Brien 2002: 67-69; Chapman 2004: 105-107; Lemos 2006: 233-34; Lanner 2006: 142-47; Jeremias 2019: 167-68; Timmer 2020: 152-53; Wessels 2020: 344-46; Noegel 2021: 319; Claassens 2021). Nineveh is depicted as a woman who is transgressing accepted norms (Berlejung 2006: 338-40). These indications are depreciative and clearly part of anti-Assyrian propaganda. I do not think that they claim to be exact descriptions of Nineveh or hint at a specific historical figure, such as queen Naqia (Cook 2017b). The images are an indication of the way in which the Assyrian presence in the levant had been experienced. The images refer to deep scars in the lives of individuals and communities. They felt misled and cheated by the intoxicating and enrapturing acts. They contain a judgment: in her robbery and greed, she, the city, trespassed a given line. This judgment functions as a motivation in two directions. It gives the author a moral base both for the woe-oracle and for the prophecy of doom.

The composition 3.1-7 is concluded by a prophecy of doom. I do not construe 3.5-7 as a later addition since these verses conceptually fit with 3.1-3 and 3.4 (contra Berlejung 2006: 337-38). Schulz (1973: 41-59) argued unconvincingly that 3.7 should be read as the opening line of a mocking-song against Nineveh. In my view, 3.7 should rather be seen as the concluding remark of 3.1-7. Besides, 3.8 opens a whole new dimension of the text. As introduction, the author repeats in 3.5 the words of the threatening speech formula (2.14) instead of the more traditional formula, 'Thus says YHWH'. In doing so, the various units are interconnected. The doom for Nineveh consists in a disconcerting act: Nineveh will be uncovered and denuded. Her shame will be visible for all. Some scholars argue that these lines are to be read as a metaphor for rape (Magdalena 1995; Spronk 1997: 123-24; O'Brien 2002: 67-69; 2004: 49; Lanner 2006: 149-50; Baumann 2012; Tuell 2016: 11; Kruger 2014: 164-70; Spronk 2018: 239-40; Wessels 2018;

2020: 344-46; Graybill 2021: 25-29; questioned by Jeremias 1970: 36-37; Renaud 1987: 313; Klopper 2003; Fabry 2006: 109-11, 194-96; Hagedorn 2011: 58-59; Cook 2016a; Dietrich 2016: 79-80; Tuell 2016: 41-45; Jeremias 2019: 173-76; Timmer 2020: 155-57; Wenyi 2021: 177). The absence of a Hebrew word for this disgusting act should be read as an act of silencing the unnamable. This silence makes it difficult to establish the exact degree of humiliation that Nineveh will meet. As a counterimage to the sexual abuse by Assyrian soldiers, Nineveh will be violated. Such a counterimage could help victims of Assyrian sexual rudeness to cope with their trauma (Klopper 2003; Christensen 2009: 344; Frechette 2016; Spronk 2018: 239-40).

Jacob Onyumbe Wenyi wrote the bitter words: 'Rape is not simply a *consequence* of war; it is part of the *strategy* of war' (Wenyi 2021: 35). These words, written in the context of the atrocities in Eastern Congo, are disgustingly true. Reports on war from all ages and places are filled with this masculine trespassing (see, e.g., Ferguson 2021; Kulik 2022).

On the other hand, the language in 3.5 might contain a reference to the customs around divorce in the texts from Hana. The wife who is sent away with the formula 'You are not my wife' has to go forth stripped and naked if she initiates a divorce or remarries (Hanley 2017; Jeremias 2019: 174-75; the text can be found at Clay 1923: Text 52; *pace* Hanley, I cannot find this stipulation in the texts from Nuzi). In that case, Nah. 3.5 would refer to a shameful and victimizing act that certainly would have been experienced as traumatic.

The lines are a metaphor that the naked truth about Nineveh will be uncovered. Above—5.3.2—a parallel with a curse from the Aramaic treaty between Mattiel, king of Arpad, and Bargayah, king of the enigmatic kingdom KTK, has already been indicated:

> [and just as a pros]ti[tute is stripped naked;
> So may the wives of Mattiel be stripped naked
> And the wives of his offspring and the wives of [his] no[bles].
> (Sefire 1 A,44)

Nineveh will be trumped by an act that uses the language of the stock phrases of the binding agreements between superior and inferior powers in the ancient Near East. The end result of the divine intervention is summarized in the words 'Nineveh is devastated!'

As with the previous and the final unit in Nahum, 3.1-7 is concluded with a question about the absence of mourners for Nineveh. Above, I already referred to a parallel with a curse in the Neo-Assyrian treaties:

> May your ghost have nobody to take care of the pouring of libations to him.
> (Succession Treaty of Esarhaddon; VTE § 47; SAA 2, 6:452)

The absence of persons to perform the mourning rites was a shameful situation in the ancient Near East. It implied that the deceased were condemned to a dreadful existence in the netherworld (see Becking 1995; Olyan 2004: 28-61).

As in Nah. 2.10, this section is framed by the idea of *ius talionis*. Nineveh gets her tricks at home. The trauma inflicted on the nations will come home to her without consolation (Wessels 2020: 345-46).

6.3.4 Comparing Capitals (3.8-19)

The third and final section offers a comparison between Nineveh and the Egyptian city No-Amon (Thebes). The conquest of that mighty city—whether or not historical—functions as a warning to the Assyrian capital. Here is my translation:

8 Are you better than No-Amon,
   situated at the streams
      waters round about her,
   as rampart a sea,
      from water her wall?
9 Cush was her might,
      Egypt, too, and without limit;
   Put and the Libyans were her helpers.
10 Even she went into exile;
      into captivity;
   even her infants were dashed in pieces
      at the corner of every street;
   For her nobles lots were cast;
      all her important men were bound in fetters.
11 You too will get drunken;
      it will get blurry;
   you too will have to seek,
      a refuge from the enemy.
12 All your fortresses are like a fig tree
      With early fruits—
   When tossed about,
      they fall into the mouth of the eater.
13 Look, the troops in your midst are like women
   To your enemies,
      the gates of your land are wide open;
   fire shall devour the bars of your gates.
14 Draw water for the siege;
   strengthen your fortresses;

go into the clay; tread the mortar;
    make strong the brick mold!
15 Certainly, the fire will devour you;
    the sword will strike you.
It will devour you like a young grasshopper.
Make yourself heavy like a young grasshopper;
    Make yourself heavy like a locust!
16 You have made your merchants more numerous
    Than the stars of the heavens.
A young grasshopper strips off oneself
    and flies away
17 Your courtiers are like locusts,
    your clerks like a swarm of grasshoppers
Who encamps on the city wall
    on a cold day—
when the sun rises, they flee away;
    no one knows its place.

18 Where are your shepherd's pastures,
    —the king of Assyria—;
        where the important ones lay themselves?
Your people are scattered on the mountains
    and no one collects them.
19 There is no healing for your fracture;
    your wound is incurable.
All who hear the message about you
    Will clap their hands over you.
For upon whom
    has not come your unceasing evil?

This unit answers the implicit question: how realistic is the prospect that Nahum paints? Would the first reaction not be: Nineveh is such a well-defended city, your prophecy could never happen? Don't you sow vain hopes with these overwrought expectations? This is of course a perennial question in cases of enduring trauma when those who suffer are promised a new future. Nahum 3.8 poses a rhetorical question to the readers.

The book of Nahum answers this question through a comparison. Nineveh (3.11-17) is compared with No-Amon (3.8-10). In the Assyrian construction of the then-recent past this almost impregnable Egyptian city had fallen prey to the onrushing Assyrian armies (but see above 5.1). The downfall of No-Amon functions as an analogy of hope (Wenyi 2021: 37-40). It is quite revealing to compare Nahum's comparison with a Neo-Assyrian astrological report. Apparently a diviner was asked whether or not the Neo-Assyrian king, most probably Ashurbanipal, should wage war against the

Cimmerians and the Manneans. In his report, the astrologer construes the visibility of the moon on the first day as a good omen:

> When Aššur, Šamaš, Nabû, and Marduk gave Kush and Egypt into the hands of the king [my lord], they plundered them [...] with the troops of the king my lord. [Gold and silver from] their treasury, as much as there was, they brought [into] your royal abode [Ni]neveh [and distributed] booty from them to his servants.
>
> In the same way (*ki-i pi-i*), may Šamaš and Mard[uk] give the Cimmerians and Man[neans], all [enem]ies who [do not fear] the king, into the hands of the king my lord; may [the king] my lord plunder them.
> (SAA 8.418: 4- Rev2).

There is a striking contrast between this report and the book of Nahum. In the Neo-Assyrian letter, the comparison with the Egyptian campaign works in favor of the Assyrian king. This is turned into a comparison in disfavor of Nineveh by Nahum.

In the name of the city No-Amon (lit. City of Amon), the second element clearly refers to the Egyptian deity Amun or Amun-Re, an Egyptian creator god and the patron deity of Thebes (Assmann 1995). It should be noted that the author of 4Q385a 17 ii:8 reads only the name Amon (see Tigchelaar 2017; Jeremias 2019: 41). There is, however, yet another possibility to read the name Amon. In 2 Kgs 21.10-25 the short reign of the Judaean king Amon (*'āmôn*) is narrated. After two years of reign, he fell prey to a conspiracy of his servants. Thereupon the conspirers were killed by the 'people of the land', who installed the eight-year-old Josiah as king in Jerusalem. Later, Josiah would reform the cult of Yhwh in Jerusalem. These dramatic events probably happened a few years before the book of Nahum came to light. No-Amon then might be a cryptic reference to Jerusalem as the city of King Amon. This playful sidestep opens the possibility that the comparison could also be between Jerusalem—as once almost conquered by the Assyrians—and Nineveh, or to the comparison between the dramatic events around the death of King Amon and Nineveh. The dramatic events lead to the unexpected end of the syncretism as promoted by Manasseh and his son. Likewise, Nineveh could meet its almost impossible and unexpected end.

Above (5.1), I have indicated the problem that the Assyrian conquest of Thebes is not mentioned in Egyptian sources and referred to the fact that the archaeology of Thebes does not indicate an Assyrian assault. In addition, it is remarkable that the image of Thebes in Nahum 3 is difficult to reconcile with the situation in Egypt. The depiction of No-Amon by Nahum does not match the Egyptian city, which was not surrounded by waters as was Nineveh. I am not convinced by the attempts of Schneider who connects these waterworks of defense for No-Amon with an abundant inundation of the Nile (Schneider 1988). It is therefore very plausible that the author of the book of Nahum dressed the Egyptian city with the gown of the topography of the Assyrian capital as Huddlestun has argued (2003). A warning against an all-too-factual reading of this passage is made by Crouch, who notes that the 'waters' not only have a topographic connotation but also a mythic background (Crouch 2009: 165-66).

A remark should be made on v. 10. Infanticide is sometimes mentioned in Neo-Assyrian reports on conquests (Dewar 2021). No mention of it, however, is made in the inscriptions of the Sargonic kings. According to Berlejung (2006: 340), murdering children of the enemy was not seen as a heroic act to be narrated. The assumed purpose of the horrible act could have been the preventing of a next generation among a rebellious people (Renz 2021: 174). On the other hand, a curse in the Succession Treaty of Esarhaddon reads:

> May Belet-ili, the lady of creation, cut off birth (*ta-lit-tu*) from your land; may she deprive your nurses of the cries of little children in the streets and squares.
> (Succession Treaty of Esarhaddon; VTE § 46; SAA 2, 6:437-39 // SAA 2, 15 T vi:9-12)

In the Hebrew Bible, the element of the death of children in Israelite and Judahite warfare occurs a few times (Hos. 10; 2 Kgs 15.16; see Crouch 2009: 168-69). The supposed infanticide by the Assyrians might be an exaggeration of the reality based on Israelite experiences. It hints at the traumatized rage of the author of the book of Nahum.

The author of Nahum makes a connection between No-Amon and Nineveh. Against Jeremias (1970: 41-43), who argues for the view that this text was originally directed against Jerusalem and redirected against Nineveh by the redactor of the book of Nahum, I would argue that his position is weak and based only on the assumption of a redactional process (see also Keller 1972). Against the view of Christensen (2009: 358), who reads vv. 10-13 as a description of the fate of Thebes, I would argue that his interpretation of *gam* as 'so it was with her (that is Thebes)' is rather fanciful (see Labuschagne 1966; Renz 2021: 165). At the level of words the repetition of the adverb *gam*, 'also; too', in vv. 10 and 11 indicates this connection (see also Wenyi 2021: 141-42). The defenselessness of the once so powerful cities is drawn in a series of images. Auxiliaries, fortified towns and outposts will no longer be of any use. Diplomacy and trade have lost their power. The once-tough warrior people are compared with women (a comparison that can no longer be made, but fits within the old Eastern vision of the male-female relations). Nineveh is summoned to arm itself against a siege, but the call will be a wasted effort. Again, the concept of *ius talionis* stands in the background (Crouch 2009: 169-72).

In a mirror image, the onrushing troops are compared with locusts. This comparison is also present in Assyrian royal inscriptions (see *CAD* E, 257 c); Johnston 2002: 38-39; Bosman 2002: 593; Berlejung 2006: 343). For instance:

> Like a spring invasion of a swarm of locusts, they were advancing towards me as a group to do battle. The dust of their feet covered the wide heavens like a heavy cloud in the deep of winter.
> (Sennacherib, Chicago/Taylor Prism RINAP 3, 22 v:56-59; see Bach 2022: 37)

In the book of Nahum, they appear in two categories (Wenyi 2021: 143-44 proposes three categories, but his last two overlap). The first group is labelled 'young grasshoppers'. As in the book of Joel, they symbolize the downfall in their bald eating (Wenyi 2021: 143-44). The irresistible actions of a group of locusts were known in reality as well as in symbols throughout the ancient Near East (see, e.g., Ugarit *KTU* 1.3 ii:9-11; 1.14 ii:51-111:1; Judg. 6.5; 7.12), including in Egypt (see Brachmańska 2021). In the hymn to Nanaya of Sargon II, this image is given:

> The evil locust which ravages the grain, the malignant grasshopper which dries up the orchards, which would cut off the regular offerings of god and goddess
> (SAA 3, 24:24-26; see Hurowitz 1993).

The hymn continues with the wish that the power of these grasshoppers may be nullified (SAA 3,4:29). In an astrological report to an unknown king, the eclipse of the moon is seen as an omen:

> If the moon is dark in Tishri: fall of a great army; there will be an attack of an enemy or of locusts [...].
> (SAA 8, 103: 10; see also SAA 10, 364: 12)

The second group is mentioned in 3.15-17. These locusts belong to a different family. They are not symbolic for the onrushing armies but stand for Nineveh and the way the Assyrians would have been eating bare the harvest of the provinces and the vassal kingdoms (Wenyi 2021: 144). Nahum refers explicitly to peddlers, officials and courtiers who abused their position for personal greed. In fact, the author sneers at the uselessness of these functionaries with their nation at war (Mankowski 2000: 96). Again, the central image is that of the concept of *ius talionis* (Bosman

2002: 359; Petersen 2002: 199; O'Brien 2004: 50; Crouch 2009: 169-72; Timmer 2020: 170-71). The harm done will return to the Assyrians. Needless to say how current this image is when you look at the recent locust plagues in the horn of Africa caused by drought, climate change and warfare. Verse 15 ends with two ironic imperatives. Nineveh is summoned to 'grow heavy' as voracious locusts do (see Pinker 2003a). The irony lies in the fact that thickening themselves will not be of any help on the day of disaster for Nineveh.

Verse 16 contains an intriguing reproach. Nineveh is accused of having 'multiplied their merchants more than the stars of heaven'. This line refers to the experience of the omnipresence of Assyrian traders in the Levant, or at least the perception of being overrun by Assyrian traders. Cat Quine made some important remarks on the comparison 'more than the stars of heaven'. She indicated an intertextual connection to the promises in the Hebrew Bible for the future of Israel as for instance in the closing lines of the bitter story of the 'binding of Isaac':

> I will indeed bless you, and I will make your offspring as numerous as the stars of heaven and as the sand that is on the seashore.
> (Gen. 22.17; see also Gen. 26.4; Exod. 32.13; Deut. 1.10; 10.22; Neh. 9.23; 1 Chr. 27.23)

I would like to add to that a parallel found in the report of the Eighth Campaign of Sargon II in which the booty taken from Urartu is said:

> to have no number like stars in the sky (*kakkabū šamê*).
> (Sargon II Eighth Campaign = RINAP 2, 65:164; see Bach 2022: 37)

The author of Nahum—through the choice of these words—accuses Nineveh for trying to be better than the God of Israel. Correctly, Quine pays attention to the use of the preposition *min* instead of k^e as in the other phrases underscoring semantically that Nineveh is seen as overdoing God. It should be remarked that this reproach directed against Nineveh has its place in a text to be read by Judaeans and not by Assyrians. Indirectly, the audience is warned not to be impressed by international trade or the Assyrian bureaucracy. In the end, God will be stronger! (Quine 2019).

The element of 'fleeing away' (3.16-17) of the 'locusts' when in danger has a counterpart in a motif in Neo-Assyrian texts. The enemies of the Assyrians are said to flee away when threatened. Various animals are named in comparison, but no locusts (see Bach 2022: 39-42).

The final unit in the book of Nahum is closed by a scornful hymn (3.18-19). This hymn has the structure of a ring composition:

A	18a-d	Question to Nineveh
B	19a-d	Observation on Nineveh
A'	19e-f	Question to Nineveh

This small unit is a cynical complaint on Nineveh seen as dead. Traditionally, a lamentation would contain references to the virtues of the deceased. Here we read elements of grimness: an incurable wound, defenselessness and the absence of consolation.

The two questions around the observation stand in parallel. The translation of the first question is problematic. With van der Woude, I construe the final word of 3.17—*'ayyām*, 'where?'—as part of the first clause of 18 (*pace*, e.g., Rudolph 1975: 181; Roberts 1991: 69.72; Nogalski 1993a: 42; Spronk 1997: 140-41; Lanner 2006: 85.160-61; Hagedorn 2011: 40; Tuell 2016: 48-49; Jeremias 2019: 200-201; Timmer 2020: 171). The word *nāmû* is not to be read as a verbal form (*pace* Roberts 1991: 76-77; Lanner 2006: 161-62; Timmer 2020: 151) but as the Assyrian loanword *nāmû/nāwû*, 'pasture', comparable to Hebrew *nāweh* (see Van der Woude 1978: 125; the argument by Jeremias 2019: 206, that this proposal is philologically 'unhaltbar', is not convincing).

The word 'shepherd' refers to either the king of Assyria (thus Van der Woude 1976: 125-26; Renaud 1987: 321; Roberts 1991: 76-77; Portuese 2020) or the deity Ashur (Lanner 2006: 161-62; Cook 2019). In both cases he failed in his protecting duties for the populace of Nineveh. He turned out to be unable to prevent his people from being scattered on the mountains. Implicitly, this stands contrary to the shepherdship of the God of Israel who eventually will protect and console his people. YHWH will gather his scattered flock.

The observation (19a-d) is full of bitterness for Nineveh. The motif of the 'incurable wound' is well known in Assyrian inscriptions, for instance in the curses written in the vassal treaties (see above). The threat uttered as warning for the client kings will return to Nineveh itself. Again, this is a trauma for a trauma. The 'clapping of the hands' is a gesture of malicious delight on the downfall of the city (see Fox 1995; Fabry 2006: 223-24; Hagedorn 2011: 63).

The phrase is reminiscent of the gesture depicted on the wall reliefs of the palace of Tiglath Pileser III. It should, however, be noted that in Assyrian texts the words *ritti rapasu*, 'to clap the hands', depicts an expression of anguish or anger, comparable to the Hebrew expression *nākâ b^{e}kap*, 'to clap in your hand', as an expression of reproof (e.g. Ezek. 6.11; see Fox 1995: 51-54). It is therefore uncertain whether the relief refers to joy over a victory or the grief after a loss.

Figure 4: Wall relief from the Palace of
Tiglath Pileser III (Barnett and Falkner 1962: 12)

The final question of the book of Nahum looks back to the past. The question is rhetorical since it exposes the malicious acts of the Neo-Assyrian Empire. Too many people suffered under the yoke of Assur. Some of these evil crimes are referred to in the book of Nahum: domination; plundering; terrorizing diplomacy; bloodshed; sorcery; bad sexual behaviour (see my analysis above and Wenyi 2021: 145-54). To the current readers of the book of Nahum, this question looks forward to human history and elucidates the inclination of people in power to abuse their might for repression and the infliction of traumatic fractures and incurable wounds on individuals and communities. The final question, however, is also a drag on all too triumphant words like in the final strophe of Byron's poem 'The Destruction of Sennacherib':

> And the widows of Ashur are loud in their wail,
> And the idols are broke in the temple of Baal;
> And the might of the Gentile, unsmote by the sword,
> Hath melted like snow in the glance of the Lord!
>   (Byron 1903: 222)

This dual view of God and his different treatment of Israel/Judah and Nineveh will be reinforced by an analysis of the opening hymn of Nahum in the next chapter.

7

Divine Duality and the Duel in History

7.1 Text and Translation

The message of the book of Nahum is clear and two-sided: hope for Judah will go hand in hand with doom for Assyria. In the three units discussed above, some hints are given as to the view why this will happen. In short, according to the author of the book of Nahum, Nineveh had overplayed her hand. She was called to be an instrument in the hands of Yhwh to punish Judah and Israel for their transgressions, but she enjoyed too much in this role and she repressed the population of Judah and Samaria (and other nations) in such a way that she is now called to order. The element that the trauma supposedly brought over Israel and Judah is a result of the trespasses against God is silenced in the book of Nahum. It is not mentioned at the surface of the text for obvious reasons. It would be far from mild to burden the traumatized with this notion. Cook has made clear—through a comparison with Josh. 24.19—that in the deeper fabric of the text this element can be read (Cook 2020). Nineveh will be punished for crossing the boundaries of the mandate given to her. Trauma will meet her for all the trauma inflicted. The opening hymn of the biblical book functions as a theological foundation for this view (1.2-8). I will first offer my translation:

2   A jealous God and an avenger is Yhwh;
        An avenger is Yhwh and a lord of grimness;
    An avenger is Yhwh to his adversaries
        and he is furious with his enemies.
3   Yhwh is long suffering but great in power,
        and Yhwh never leaves unpunished.

    In storm wind and in whirlwind is his way,
        and the cloud cover is the dust for his feet.
4   he bawls against the sea and dries her up,
        and all the rivers he dehydrates;

Bashan and Carmel have withered,
    and the bloom of the Lebanon has withered.
5   Mountains tremble for him,
        and the hills melt away;
    the earth wails before him,
        —the mainland and all its residents—.
6   Who can stand before his wrath?
        Who can stand up before his burning anger?
    His rage is poured out like fire,
        the rocks break to pieces before him.

7   Yhwh is good,
        He is a shelter on the day of anxiety;
    knowing those
        who seek refuge with him,
8   but with an overflowing flood,
        he completely destroys her place
            by eagerly pursuing his enemies into darkness.

This unit consists in three parts that form a concentric symmetry:

A   1.2-3a   Divine wrath and long-suffering
X   1.3b-6   God's coming to judgment
A'   1.7-8   God is a saviour as well as a destroyer.

A similar view has been proposed by other scholars, but without the concept of a concentric symmetry (Dietrich 2016: 42; Timmer 2020: 70-73).

7.2 Seven Attributes/Virtues/Enduring Characteristics

The first unit is a restricted theology in hymnic form. Although clear on the character of God, the text is permeated with tension and mystery. There is a riddle when it comes to the question Who is who? Who are, for instance, the enemies? To whom is God long-suffering? In a series of seven virtues, the author gives testimony of the experience with God. I will discuss them. I prefer the word 'virtues' over the more philosophical 'attributes' as the rendering of the concept of the *middôt*. In my opinion, the word 'virtue' accounts for their relational character. Next to that, I do not construe these 'virtues' as separate divine dimensions but as interconnected indications on the enigmatic God (see Baumann 2005: 63).

1. He is a jealous God. This expression is attested elsewhere six times in the Hebrew Bible in the context of covenant clauses (Exod. 20.5; 34.14;

Deut. 4.24; 5.9; 6.15; Josh. 24.19). In all these texts there is a connection with the prohibition to venerate other gods. The jealousy of Yʜᴡʜ is an expression of his love and grounded in the special relationship with Israel. As liberator of the Hebrew slaves out of the bondage of Egypt, Yʜᴡʜ claims monolatry by the Israelites out of gratitude. Out of love for his people, God is jealous when they leave him for another god (see also Renaud 1963; Roberts 1991: 49-50; Baumann 2005: 64-69; Tuell 2016: 22; Jeremias 2018: 221-22; 2019: 63-66; Timmer 2020: 74-75; Renz 2021: 67). He is so fond of this people that he does not want them to abandon him. That is the one side of divine jealousy. The exiles—both the Assyrian and the Babylonian—are interpreted by the writers of the Hebrew Bible as final acts of divine jealousy. The other side of jealousy came to the fore in texts written around the Babylonian Exile. In these texts the noun 'jealousy' is not connected with punishment but with salvation for the people in humiliating distress. The mechanics of jealousy can best be sketched with the use of a triangle: God—Israel—other nations. God will be angry with Israel when it walks after the deities (and the social and economic code) of the other nations. God will, however, become angry with the other nations when they repress, tyrannize and humiliate Israel (see Becking 2013). At this early moment in the unfolding text of Nahum it is not yet clear which side of jealousy is referred to.

2. He is an avenger. In the biblical idiom, the verb *nāqam*, 'to take revenge', refers an act that 'restores the proper relationship within a community and/or with God' (Heschel 1962: 4-6, 62-64; De Vries 1966: 478; Peels 1995; O'Brien 2002: 48; Baumann 2005: 69-76; Christensen 2009: 219-22; Tuell 2016: 22-23; Jeremias 2018: 222-24; Timmer 2020: 75-76; Timmer 2021: 161-62). Jeremias, correctly, argues that 'being a revenger' is not a fundamental unchangeable attribute in God, but always presented as a possibility to react to trespasses of whatever kind (Jeremias 2019: 66-68). The way in which the balance in a relationship is restored in biblical narratives is—in modern eyes—often quite rude and inhumane, especially when presented as an act of God. There is generally shivering when reading a story like the one in which the prophet Elisha takes revenge on forty-two bullying children by having them killed by a bear from the woods (2 Kgs 2.23-24). The Hebrew Bible gives an unrestrained testimony on divine revenge. This virtue of God has two sides. In a series of texts, God's revenge is presented as punishment for the breach of the covenant relationship by Israel (e.g. Lev. 26.14-17; Isa. 1.24; Jer. 5.9; 9.8; Ezek. 24.8). Next to that there are texts testifying God as taking revenge on the adversaries of Israel, for instance in the song of Moses (Deut. 32) and in oracles of salvation in the book of Jeremiah

(Jer. 46.10; 50.15, 28; 51.6, 11, 36). In all these passages, divine revenge is never seen as arbitrary but always based in the love of God. At this early moment in the unfolding text of Nahum it is not yet clear which side of revenge is implied.

3. **He is lord of grimness.** In this clause God is named a Baal: *ba'al ḥēmâ*, which should be construed as expressing a *genitivus qualitatis* and rendered as 'a grim lord'. The author gives a wink to the name of the Canaanite deity Baal. The noun *ḥēmâ* is one of the ten Hebrew terms for 'wrath'. Divine wrath should be understood in the framework of the relationship between YHWH and Israel. As with the previous two virtues, 'grimness' has two sides. Jeremiah 4.4 narrates that God's grimness will be awoken when the inhabitants of Jerusalem do not turn back from their evil conduct. Ezekiel 25.14, 17 indicate that the grimness of God could—in protection—also be targeted at the enemies of Israel. At this stage of the book of Nahum, it is not yet clear whether this grimness will be helpful or disastrous (see Baumann 2005: 76-78; Jeremias 2009; Jeremias 2018: 224-25).

The notion of 'divine wrath' in the book of Nahum can be construed in two ways. The fury of God could be directed toward the Israelites or to the threatening enemy as clarified in the following figures (see also Scoralik 2002: 196):

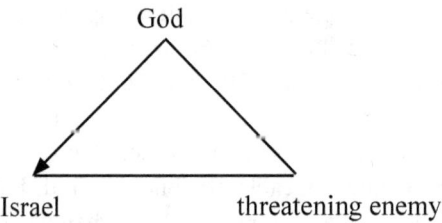

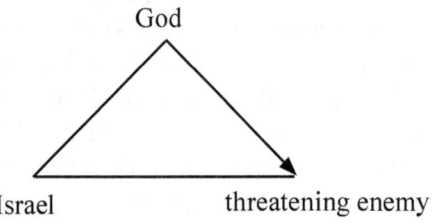

In the first figure, the divine fury is directed toward Israel; in the second, toward the enemy. As the discourse develops within the text of Nahum, it becomes clear that the 'divine wrath' needs to be interpreted as a protective wrath. Almost everywhere else in the Hebrew Bible, the wrath of God is directed against Israel as a punishing fury. This element is silenced in the book of Nahum (see Cook 2020). Nahum 1 is the great exception to this concept: here the divine is redirected toward the conqueror who will be conquered (see Jeremias 2009).

4. He is furious. In biblical Hebrew, there are two homonymous verbs *nāṭar* (see Clines, *DCH* 5, 679; Spronk 1997: 35; Baumann 2005: 78-79). The first, with the meaning 'to keep, guard' occurs four times in the Song of Songs; for instance, 'they made me guardian of the vineyards; my own vineyard I did not guard'. The second verb, 'to be angry, furious', is attested five times in the Hebrew Bible. Some scholars construe this verb as an ellipsis for *nāṭar 'āp*, (e.g. Kraus 1973: 703); others see a parallel with Akkadian *nadāru*, 'to rage' (*CAD* N1: 59-61; see Cathcart 1973a: 43; Roberts 1991: 43). Once a human is the subject (Lev. 19.18), but elsewhere God is seen as the one who is furious. In Ps. 103.9 and Jer. 3.5, 12 it is stated that God's fury will not endure forever. In Nah. 1.3 God's fury is directed against 'his adversaries'. In Nah. 1.2 *nāṭar* functions as a specification of God's revenge (Spronk 1997: 35; Renz 2021: 68-69). At this point in the text, it is still unclear who the objects of God's fury are.

5. He is long-suffering. There is an intertextual relation with the old confession:

> Yhwh, Yhwh,
> a God merciful and gracious, long-suffering,
> and abounding in steadfast love and faithfulness.
> (Exod. 34.6-7; see also Num. 14.18; Joel 2.13; Jon. 4.2: Ps. 86.15; 103.8; 145.8; Neh. 9.17; see the outline in Timmer 2020: 77)

This confession expresses the core testimony of hope, nearness and guidance (Brueggemann 1997: 268-87). This virtue brings to life a different keynote than the previous ones. The character of the relation between God and humans is in the first place positive. Already at the surface, there is a reference to God's help for people and not to his punishment against living beings. The Hebrew expression *'erek 'appayîm* literally means 'long of nose' or 'long of rage'. This has been developed into 'slow to wrath', which means that God keeps his wrath to himself and hence gives humans a chance to repent. God allows humans time and space. God's leniency is the basis of human hope. To whom this hope will be given is not yet clear in the development of the text.

6. He is great in power. In the confession alluded to by the author of Nahum, the word 'long-suffering' is followed by *w^erab ḥesed*, 'full of steadfast love'. Nahum bursts through the succession of equal elements by plac-

ing *ûgᵉdôl koᵃh*, 'great of strength' after 'long-suffering'. This evokes a contradiction that leads to the adversative translation of the conjunction: 'Yhwh is long suffering but great in power'. Some scholars see this contradiction as a problem to be solved either by supposing that *ḥesed*, 'steadfast love', had been the original reading (e.g. Elliger 1951: 3) or by striking *'erek 'appayîm*, 'long-suffering' (especially Humbert 1926: 266). In my view, there is no problem, since Nah. 1.3 contains a twofold testimony. On the one hand, God is long-suffering, but on the other hand, he is great of strength. He possesses the power to actually carry out his revenge and wrath (see also De Vries 1966: 408; Cook 2016b; Timmer 2020: 79-80). Yhwh's great power should be seen as directed against the same group that will be terrified by his avenging wrath. To whom his long-suffering will be directed is not yet clear in the development of the text.

7. He never leaves unpunished. These words occur twice as an extension to the confession mentioned above (Exod. 34.7; Num 14.18). They also are attested in the Decalogue: the transgression of using the name of God in vain will not be left unpunished. These words expose a side of God that many modern readers would like to ignore. They need to be read in their context and not be interpreted as an unchangeable attribute of God that fits all circumstances leading to a one-sided and gloomy image of God. In the context of the book of Nahum they communicate that God certainly will take revenge. To whom this revenge is directed will become clear in the rest of the book. It should be noticed that these works also contain an element of hope for those who became victim of other humans' transgressions.

All in all, this image of Yhwh is to be seen as an appropriation of the confession-like phrase in Exod. 34.6-7 to the traumatic perception of the Assyrian domination as a yoke. In these desperate and hopeless times, the author of Nahum reverts to the shared tradition of Israel which is bent to an image of God that could be the starting point of a new future (see also Renaud 1987: 279-80; Spieckermann 1990; Brueggemann 1997: 220-21, 268-72; O'Brien 2002: 48-49; 2004: 34-35; Scoralik 2002; Franz 2003; Baumann 2005: 82-94; Christensen 2009: 17; Lane 2010: 68-110; Jeremias 2015: 285-95; 2018: 226-28; 2019: 71-74; Tuell 2016: 23; Cook 2016b; Collins 2019: 154-57; Renz 2021: 69-71; Wenyi 2021: 77-78, 110-15). The hymnic presentation of these seven divine characteristics opens a window on divine duality: God is seen both as an avenger and as a good God (Garber 2008: 288-89; Spronk 2018: 243). This duality, however, evokes a tension. If the book of Nahum would have ended at this point, the reader would have been left in uncertainty: Who will be punished? Who will be saved?

In relation to the rest of the book it becomes clear that the impending fates of Nineveh and Israel are seen as an effectuation of God's avenging love for his people.

It should be noted that I am not convinced by the as such intriguing proposal of Lauren Lanner to interpret these opening lines as a reference to three deities: *yhwh*, *'ēl* and *ba'al* (Lanner 2006: 101-104). The appropriation of the creed from Exodus 34 situates the hymnic theology of Nah. 1.2-3a in a Yahwistic context. Besides, I read *ba'al ḥēmâ* as the expression of a genitive of quality (see Becking 1995: 287) and construe *'ēl* as a noun, 'god', and not as a name for a deity. At best, there is a hidden polemic in this unit (see also Spronk 1997: 35).

7.3 Divine Epiphany

The middle part of the hymn contains a description of a divine epiphany (1.3b-6). This genre is well known in ancient Near Eastern texts as well as in the Hebrew Bible (Jeremias 1965; 2019: 74-83; Scriba 1995; Savran 2003; Tuell 2016: 23-25; DeLapp 2018; Wenyi 2021: 121-28). In these texts, the enormous forces of nature are depicted as a side-effect of the apparition of the divine. The description of the epiphany in Nahum 1 has a traditional design:

1.3b   The apparition of YHWH
1.4-5 The side-effects in nature
1.6   Concluding question

It should be remarked that the third element does not occur in other texts. This is a specificum for Nahum that forms a hinge to the two surrounding elements.

Nahum 1.4-5 describes with traditional imagery the effects in the world of nature of the apparition of God. I will not dwell on the abundance of analogies of these images in Sumerian, Akkadian and Ugaritic texts. That enumeration would take too much space and besides can be found in the literature mentioned above. I will make one exception since it leads to a different translation. Klaas Spronk referred to a parallel with a hymn for Adad:

> In the Lord's anger the heavens will shake,
> In Adad's anger the earth will wail (*inassu*),
> the great mountains will crumble.
> (IV R 28:2; Rawlinson 1875: 81; Zimmern 1905: 12; Jeremias 1965: 78-79, 89-90; Loewenstamm 1980: 183; Spronk 1997: 43; Christensen 2009: 188-90)

Although a translation of *inassu* with 'he will tremble' would result in a beautiful parallelism with the trembling of the mountains in Nah. 1.5, it should be noted that the word *inassu* is to be construed as a form of the Akkadian verb *nasāsu*, 'to sing, wail, complain' (*CAD* N2: 23-24). By implication, the phrase in Nah. 1.5 depicts the reaction of the earth—and its inhabitants—to the trembling of the mountains. This implies that there is no need to add a noun *qôl*, 'voice', to the original text (contra Rudolph 1975: 150).

Of more importance are the three levels of meaning that are hidden in the text of Nah. 1.3b-5.

1. *Mythological.* The bawling against the sea is connected with the conflict with the evil powers that hide in the waters. See for instance the conflict between Baal and the sea-god Yammu in the texts from Ugarit or the victory of the Babylonian deity Marduk over the sea-dragon Tiamat in *Enuma Elish* (see the remarks in Crouch 2009: 160-64). In the New Testament it is told how Jesus subdues the angry sea (Matt. 8.26 // Luke 8.24). The theme of the withering of agricultural areas is part of the cyclical view in the ancient Near East. The death and resurrection of the deity finds a parallel in the changing of the seasons. In the Hebrew Bible, this withering is seen as a sign of God's absence and his relinquishing of meddling in human history. In a great variety of ancient Near Eastern texts, the quaking of the earth is presented as a grim act of the head of the local pantheon, for instance in Ugarit and Mesopotamia.
2. *Agrarian.* The economy of Israel and Judah was mainly agrarian. Only a few persons worked in the administration or the trade. This implies that the population was directly dependent on the mildness of the climate and the regular change of seasons. The features in nature described in Nah. 1.4-5, reflect the perennial threat of existence. A period of drought resulted in a meager crop and hence hunger. An earthquake destroyed the carefully constructed water supply for the acres and the terraces. Bashan, Carmel and the Lebanon were proverbially rich agricultural areas (see for instance Amos 4.1). When even those areas withered, a real disaster had hit the country. All forces of nature mentioned caused harm and trauma.
3. *Military.* The four agrarian elements with a mythological background function, in addition, as a metaphor that is clarified in chs. 2 and 3 of the book of Nahum (see also Johnston 2002: 29-32, 37-38; O'Brien 2002: 49-50). The forces of nature stand for the devastating forces of the military apparatus. The imagery in 1.4-5 is a prelude for the later trauma of

Nineveh (and because of the fact that the Assyrians had traumatized the Judaeans and Israelites).

This description of the divine appearance is a functional part of the hymn in Nahum 1. God's theophany is a result of his anger (*pace* Nogalski 1993b: 105-106). This textual unit is concluded by a question. This question contains two elements: the actual question as well as the circumstances in which the question is posed. The connection is syntactically made by the use of stativic *qāṭal*-forms that imply a translation with 'who can then stand?' This question refers to the moment in time when God will appear. The wider literary context makes clear that that will be a time of divine grimness, revenge (for some) and long-suffering (for others; see Jeremias 1965: 31-33, 125; Roberts 1991: 51-52; Timmer 2020: 81-85).

7.4 Shelter and Destruction

The final section of the hymn of Nahum, too, is grounded in a two-sided idea. Verse 7 praises the goodness of God, while v. 8 presents the image of disaster and downfall. God is seen as 'good' and 'ominous' at the same time.

'Goodness' is not so much a divine attribute in the same way as a 'red tomato' informs about the color of the vegetable. God's goodness is to be seen as a basic attitude in his encounters with human beings. It is a word people thankfully use in trying to describe their experience in life. The word is like the sum total of positively valued events behind which God is supposed. In Nah. 1.7 this testimony is stretched to the future: God will be good at the day of anxiety (the proposal by Lanner 2006: 104-107 to render *yôm ṣārâ* with 'the day of a female adversary, or a rival deity' has no clear lexicographic support). That day will be a day of change within history on which some people will be waylaid and cornered, while others will be saved. Within the literary context of the book of Nahum that day will mark the end of the traumatizing oppression and bring the former oppressor into anguish and anxiety (Brueggemann 1997: 272-73). On the other hand, God will make an end to the enemies of his beloved even by 'eagerly pursuing' them into darkness. The word *yᵉraddep* functions as a resultative piel (Jeremias 2019: 51; *pace* Christensen 2009: 200, who construes the form to be an *intensivus*). 'Darkness' is to be seen as a euphemism for the obscurity of 'death' or the 'netherworld' (Van der Woude 1978: 87). Which 'enemy' and 'beloved' are referred to is clarified in chs. 2 and 3 of the book of Nahum (see Jeremias 2018: 228-30; 2019). In other word: God's enemies will be driven into oblivion.

7.5 The Conceptual Coherence of the Hymn of Nahum

As I hope to have shown, there is a clear literary and conceptual connection between the three elements of the hymn of Nahum, although at first sight the parts seem to be unconnected, having a variety of literary backgrounds (confession, epiphany, prophecy of doom and salvation; see also Renaud 1987: 275-77; Timmer 2020: 70-73). Above, section 5.3.2, I have remarked that the memory of the Adad curse from the succession treaty of Esarhaddon (VTE § 47; SAA 2, 6:440-42) functions as a bracket in the hymn of Nahum holding the parts together. In the middle part of the hymn of Nahum, the epiphany, the opening clause of the Adad curse, is referred to, while in the final part of the hymn a memory of the second clause of the Adad curse can be found.

Summarized in one sentence, the coherent message of the hymn can be described as follows: God appears for judgment in the midst of a historical and human crisis (B) because he is full of wrath and of love (A) and will be a shelter for some and a destroyer for others in that ordeal (A′). In doing so, an end will be made to the ongoing trauma in Israel, Judah, and all over whom has come an unceasing trauma (see also Jeremias 1965: 31-33; Keller 1972: 418-19; Van der Woude 1978: 79-87; Deissler 1984: 206-207; Spronk 1997: 21; Christensen 2009: 219-24; Cook 2016b; Timmer 2020: 85-90). I therefore doubt the view of Seybold (1989) that the hymn was added to the older soldiers' songs to make them more acceptable for religious purposes (see also Spronk 1997: 15). Within the idea of the *ius talionis*, a new trauma will come up this time among the inhabitants of Nineveh. The moral problem of this 'trauma' for a 'trauma' will be discussed in the final chapter—although I do not have a rounded and well-considered answer to that question (see also De Vries 1966; O'Brien 2002: 52).

8

The (Im)Morality of 'an Eye for an Eye'

9.1 8.1 Some Thoughts

My reading of the book of Nahum has made a few things clear. First, that the text is based on the idea of *ius talionis*. This concurs with the observation of Berlejung that the author—and in her view the later redactors—of the biblical book inverted the heroic language from Assyrian royal inscriptions by redirecting the images against Nineveh (Petersen 2002: 199; Berlejung 2006; see also Garber 2008; Wessels 2014). The *ius talionis* principle from the ancient Near East expresses the concept of reciprocity (Otto 1994: 73-81; Crouch 2009: 169-72). The compensation for a transgression should be equal to the transgression. The idea is phrased at various instances in the Hebrew Bible, for instance at Lev. 24.19-20:

> Anyone who maims another shall suffer the same injury in return: fracture for fracture, eye for eye, tooth for tooth; the injury inflicted is the injury to be suffered. (NRSV; see also Jub. 4.31-32)

The idea, however, is not restricted to the Hebrew Bible. The principle is also found in the Babylonian Code of Hammurabi (1750 BCE):

> If a son strikes his father, his hands shall be hewn off.
> If a man put out the eye of another man, his eye shall be put out.
> If he breaks another man's bone, his bone shall be broken.
>   (Codex Hammurabi, 195-97)

In Roman law, this principle has been adapted. Although the principle was widely executed, already the early law-summary *Lex Duodecim Tabularum* made a variety of restrictions and adjustments to the principle (Twelve Tables; see Tellegen-Couperus 1993).

The concept becomes morally complicated when confused with the idea of taking the law into your own hands. In those cases there is no brake on revenge. Doing to the other what he or she would have done to you inevitably leads to a spiral of violence and vendetta that seems unstoppable (see Wenyi 2021: 171, for the whirlwind of vengeance in Eastern Congo). In such a situation, there will be only losers and victims in an all-round traumatized world. Or phrased with the words of Mahatma Gandhi (see Cortright 2015): an eye for an eye will make the whole world blind.

This is, in my opinion, the point that Jesus makes in the Sermon on the Mount:

> You have heard that it was said,
> 'An eye for an eye and a tooth for a tooth'.
> But I say to you,
> 'Do not resist the one who is evil. But if anyone slaps you on the right cheek, turn to him the other also.'
> (Matt. 5.38-39 ESV; see also Rom. 12.14-21).

In these words, the concept of retaliation is superseded by the command of non-resistance. In the background of these early Christian writings stands the belief that if revenge is necessary, it can only be executed by God (Marcus 2023).

This is in line with the ideas of retribution as expressed in the ancient Near Eastern texts mentioned above. With the line 'an eye for an eye' (and parallels) the Codex Hammurabi as well as the Hebrew Bible gives an indication of the penalty that may be imposed by a court and by no means a license for individuals to take revenge for harm done to them.

The author of the book of Nahum transposes this concept to the dimension of history. One party has inflicted another party with great trauma. God as judge determines the penalty and also carries it out. The impending trauma for Nineveh is based not on direct human acts of revenge but on a divine decision based in the jealousy of God. This is all nice and clear—to some degree—but what kind of God would justifiably punish violence with more violence (Timmer 2021: 157)?

The second item to be mentioned here is the mere fact that the book of Nahum forces open the silence. Silence and the inability to speak about the terrifying events are very common effects of trauma. What had happened was too ghastly to give words to, and the wounds in the personal memory were too disquieting to be touched upon (Liem 2007). Nevertheless, giving words to trauma could be a start to heal the scars. In opening the silence, Nahum offered a way out of the position of grief albeit by announcing acts that would lead to new forms of trauma (Herman 1997). The point in case could also be clarified by referring to the term 'dissimulation'. This is the phenomenon that a person or a community does not want to face the trauma and hence presents the symptoms to himself and those around him as less serious than they really are. This concealment of thoughts and feelings is a defensive strategy by which a person or a community wants to prevent too much attention and hopes to live a life as normal as possible. In the end, dissimulation is counterproductive. The veiling of the true feelings is a pseudo-protection, because one day the trauma claims its rights and explodes into sadness deeper than thought possible (see Rogers 2008).

8.2 Two Final Questions without a Clear Answer

The two remaining questions are: (1) What does this concept of 'an eye for an eye' mean for the current victims of trauma? (2) What does it tell us about God or, more carefully, what image of God is Nahum presenting?

Can the concept of Nahum be transposed one-on-one to the twenty-first century? That would be—in my view—an almost impossible endeavour. The only thing that can be transferred is the underlying hope that is present in these three chapters from the Hebrew Bible. Even today, people can hope for an end to their misery.

It should be noted that Nahum's way out of trauma is not the only route that could be taken. On this other pathway three stations are of importance: mourning, coping and healing.

People suffering from trauma are helped by the listening ear of the silent other who opens the sufferer to really bewail the trauma and step over the threshold that was installed inside to stash away the trauma (Van der Kolk 2014; Huber 2023). From the multitude of examples and stories on this healing ear, I refer to the report on the way in which Australian soldiers, veterans and their families were consoled in the 'Warrior Welcome Home retreats'. The care of a listening and supportive community helped the traumatized on their way to healing (see West and Cronshaw 2023). Being this ear is something every human being is morally conscripted to. People suffering from trauma are also helped when their traumatic experience is not waved away. This point is formulated in a pointed way by Mihelič in his early post–World War II article (Mihelič 1948).

Coping is a process by which human beings encounter the troubles and trauma that disrupted their lives. Coping generally is defined in psychological terms (see Lazarus and Folkman 1984). The aim of coping is to reduce stress and to find ways for acceptance. Psychologists have detected hundreds of different ways in which humans try to cope with infringements on their lives. In this variety three foci can be seen.

- Sometimes people concentrate on accepting the disaster.
- Sometimes people concentrate on knowing as many facts as possible that caused the disaster.

- Sometimes people concentrate on the emotions that were aroused and released as a result of the disruption. In most cases, however, people choose a strategy that combines these three approaches (Weiten and Lloyd 2008).

Quite often, coping has a religious dimension (Kwilecki 2004). The role of religion in the first approach is apparent. Nevertheless, this acceptance is often disputed and leads to a reframing of the image of the deity. In modern times this quite often includes a farewell to the theistic image of God as omniscient and omnipresent in favour of a more personal and vulnerable image.

Healing is a complex and lengthy process. Although wounds can heal, often—if not always—a scar remains. Healing from a trauma requires patience and the courage to step over barriers, even if one enters an unfamiliar country. Healing from trauma requires hope against despair. And even then, a trauma can be lifelong and be passed on to the next generation(s) (see, e.g., Schwab 2010).

And what about God? It is relatively easy to make the observation that in the framework of that time, the words of the book of Nahum 'function as an attempt to help those suffering from the Assyrian atrocities cope with their feelings of despair. Nahum comforts his readers by describing YHWH as a god who is superior to the powerful Assyrians' (Spronk 2018: 241; compare Keller 1972; Johnston 2001b: 436; 2002: 45; Bosman 2002; Maré and Serfontein 2009; Timmer 2020: 61-62; Renz 2021: 57-58; Wenyi 2021: 170-75). It is possible to agree with that statement as a description of the past. The same holds for the view of Walter Brueggemann. He is willing to accept the violence of God because (1) it saves the lives of many powerless people in a world dominated by violence; (2) talking about a violent God is countertestimony to helpless people; and (3) divine violence is always a form of counterviolence (Brueggemann 1997: 230-76). There are, however, two problems with such images of God in a twenty-first-century context.

First, can we accept the image of a God full of revenge and violence, as comes to the fore in announcement of Nineveh's rape (3.4-7; see O'Brien 2002: 104-28; 2004: 50-51; Dietrich 2016: 25-27; Wessels 2018, 2020; Jeremias 2019: 89; Woody 2019; Graybill 2021: 28)? Do we in the twenty-first century CE have to believe in a God who punishes every punisher? Would that morally be appropriate? Immediately, the question arises regarding the connection between divine love and the concept of 'an eye for an eye'. I have no answer to these questions on theodicy, only a few remarks. (1) Frechette has argued that the violent language against enemies in the Psalms as such can have a healing function (Frechette 2014). I would, however, add to that: as long as this language is not seen as a model worthy of imitating in human actions. (2) I disagree with the view of Renz (2021: 57-58, 191-92), who, out of pastoral motifs, tries to downplay the rude side of God by referring to divine grace and love as revelated for instance at the cross and in the resurrection. In my work as a pastor, I have experienced that such sincere and heartfelt remarks sound hollow in confrontation with sorrow and trauma. They only seal the wounds temporarily. (3) Are these real questions or only ideas within an armchair theology (see also the warning in Tuell 2016: 11-12)? Are these questions put between the confusing mess of a muddled world or are they only something to pass the time in the luxury of an unbroken existence? Or, as Mihelič already formulated:

> It is my opinion that if the critics of Nahum had lived in the last decade and witnessed the brutality that had been visited upon the helpless people in the European and Asiatic concentration camps, that they would rather have joined their voices with Nahum in his joy over the fall of the 'bloody city', than have condemned his righteous indignation in the comfort and the security of their ivory towers. (Mihelič 1948: 199-200)

This opens the eye for the acceptance that pacifism—although worth emulating as such—can be a luxury position of those who live privileged and far away from the seats of war with their cruelty. Living away from the trenches of today it is easy to condemn all forms of violence. I made a remarkable observation during the war in Ukraine. When the flames of terror and trauma arrived at our doorsteps, many people who abhorred war reversed their view into an opposite position by pleading to support Ukraine with weapons of war. Both views, although opposite, share the feature of being a primary reaction that could have been thought over. The book of Nahum, then, is like a mirror in which pacifist readers are confronted with their own hidden violence and war supporters with the consequences of violence. Sometimes hate can be a virtue, but love is a greater virtue (Soloveichik 2003).

The second problem is connected with the question of how to deal with the misogynistic character of God's revenge in the book of Nahum? The literary structure as well as the conceptual coherence of the book is held in a 'patriarchal fishbowl' (O'Brien 2002: 103). Women are presented as prostitutes who will be punished with divine sexual abuse for their evil deeds. Women are presented as the less important part of a married couple. This is problematic in a religious argument that sees Scripture as source and norm for faith and behaviour. Within such a discourse the book of Nahum can be read as an invitation for men to act in an abusive way (see, e.g., Magdalene 1995; O'Brien 2002: 87-103; Wessels 2018). History is full of this dangerous and traumatizing form of *imitatio dei* (see, e.g., Portier-Young 2012). Being aware of this Scripture-sanctioned virile behaviour—Tenakh, Bible or Quran—and the trauma it inflicts in the lives of so many women, I would propose to read the misogynistic character of God as a warning. The book of Nahum then is like a mirror in which male readers are confronted with their own ugly faces and immoral conduct.

8.3 Open End

There is a time for revenge and a time for forgiveness. A time to listen and a time to speak. A time to weep and a time to laugh. A time to mourn and a time to dance. But there is never a time to renounce or reject trauma or a time for unlimited vengeance. In her astonishing book about the conduct of the allied nations in postwar Germany, Freda Utley sketches the generally silenced atrocities that Americans conducted out of revenge on German civilians. In doing so, new wounds were installed (Utley 1949; see also Minear 1971). I read her book as a warning to all who are triumphant in conflicts not to translate their victory into a fury that will bring the values of civilization at risk. A comparable tendency of reckless retribution in the post–Marshal Tito years is depicted by Volkan (1998).

All these considerations indicate that I do not have a ready answer. What I hope is that people of good will join hands and move toward a world without trauma. As Julia O'Brien phrased so wonderfully:

> A balanced ethical response to the Book of Nahum is a simultaneous yes and no—yes to the belief that tyrants stand under the judgment of God and no to taking pleasure in sexual violation, humiliation, and death, and no to any response to evil—including the reader's own—that perpetuates the very ideology of brutality that it seeks to oppose. (O'Brien 2004: 51)

In his *Theologie des Alten Testaments*, Jörg Jeremias makes an intriguing remark on the boundaries of divine anger: various texts in the Hebrew Bible give witness of the conviction 'that God is in control over his anger and set it firm, unbreachable border posts' (Jeremias 2015: 295). I read these 'border-posts' as made out of justice, $ṣ^e dāqâ$. God's anger cannot cross this line. He is bound and restricted by his own rules for a just world. By implication, human revenge is set border-posts, being bound and restricted by righteousness and fairness, by *ubuntu,* and by the concept that the other too is a member of the family of women and men (see differently phrased Collins 2019: 147-70; Wenyi 2021: 167-79; Marcus 2023). The taking into account of these border-posts will make the difference between a revengeful retribution turning into an unstoppable vendetta and retribution as just desert (see on this distinction Gerber and Jackson 2013).

I would like to round off with a quote from an ancient Lament on the destruction of Ur from the early second millennium BCE:

> May that dreadful, stormy day—like rain that has fallen—never come back again.
> May that dreadful, stormy day—that struck down the people—be utterly undone.
> May it be locked up—as if by a door, barred against the night.
> May that dreadful, stormy day not be given a place in treasured memory.
> (Lament on Ur: 411-414; Kramer 1940: 68-69; Samet 2014: 29-30; Schaudig 2019: 1)

Bibliography

Adam, A.B.
   1995   *The Vernacular Press and the Emergence of Modern Indonesian Consciousness (1855–1913)* (Ithaca, NY: Cornell University Press).

Aigner, P.
   2017   *Migrationssoziologie* (Wiesbaden: Springer Fachmedien).

Albenda, P.
   1974   'Lions on Assyrian wall reliefs', *JANES* 6: 22-33.

Alexander, J.C.
   2012   *Trauma: A Social Theory* (Cambridge: Polity).

Al-Rawi, F.N.H.
   1985   'Nabopolassar's Restoration Work on the Wall Imgur-Enlil at Babylon', *Iraq* 47: 1-13.

Arneth, M.
   2000   *'Sonne der Gerechtigkeit'. Studien zur Solarisierung der Jahwe-Religion im Lichte von Psalm 72* (BZAbR, 1) (Wiesbaden, Harrassowitz Verlag).

Assmann, J.
   1988   'Kollektives Gedächtnis und kulturelle Identität', in *Kultur und Gedächtnis* (stw 724) (ed. J. Assmann and T. Hölscher; Frankfurt a. M.: Suhrkampf): 9-19.
   1995   *Egyptian Solar Religion in the New Kingdom: Re, Amun and the Crisis of Polytheism* (London: Routledge).

Aster, S.Z.
   2015   'An Assyrian *bīt mardīte* near Tel Hadīd?', *JNES* 74. 281-88.
   2018   'Treaty and Prophecy: A Survey of Biblical Reactions to Neo-Assyrian Political Thought', in *The Southern Levant under Assyrian Domination* (ed. S.Z. Aster and A. Faust; University Park, PA: Eisenbrauns, 2018): 89-117.
   2019   'Sargon in Samaria—Unusual Formulations in the Royal Inscriptions and their Value for Historical Reconstruction', *JAOS* 139: 591-610.

Aster, S.Z., and A. Faust
   2015   'Administrative Texts, Royal Inscriptions and Neo-Assyrian Administration in the Southern Levant: The View from the Aphek-Gezer Region', *Orientalia* 84: 292-308.

Bach, J.
   2022   'Similes as a Literary Means of Narrative Identity Construction in Neo-Assyrian Royal Narrative Texts', in *The King as a Nodal Point of Neo-Assyrian Identity* (ed. J. Bach and S. Fink; Kasion, 8; Münster: Zaphon): 29-79.

Bär, J.
   1996   *Der assyrische Tribut und seine Darstellung: eine Untersuchung zur imperialen Ideologie im neuassyrischen Reich* (AOAT, 243; Neukirchen-Vluyn: Neukirchener Verlag).

Bagg, A.M.
2010 'Interaktionsformen zwischen Nomaden und Sesshaften in Palästina anhand neuassyrischer Quellen', *WdO* 40: 190-215.

Barkay, G., A.G. Vaughn, M.J. Lundberg and B. Zuckerman
2004 'The Amulets from Ketef Hinnom: A New Edition and Evaluation', *BASOR* 334: 41-71.

Barnett, R.D., and M. Falkner
1962 *The Sculptures of Ashur-nasir-apli II (883–859 B.C), Tiglath-pilesar (745–727 B.C), Esarhaddon (681–669 B.C) from the Central and South-West Palaces at Nimrud* (London: British Museum Press).

Baumann, G.
2005 *Gottes Gewalt im Wandel: traditionsgeschichtliche und intertextuelle Studien zu Nahum 1, 2-8* (WMANT, 108; Neukirchen-Vluyn: Neukirchener Verlag).
2012 'Nahum: The Just God as Sexual Predator', in *Feminist Biblical Interpretation: A Compendium of Critical Commentary on the Books of the Bible and Related Literature* (ed. L. Schottroff and M.-Th. Wacker; Grand Rapids, MI: W.B. Eerdmans): 433-42.

Becker, H.
2021 'Pigment Nomenclature in the Ancient Near East, Greece, and Rome', *Archaeological and Anthropological Sciences* 14: #20, https://link.springer.com/content/pdf/10.1007/s12520-021-01394-1.pdf.

Becking, B.
1977 *De hymne van Nahum en de literaire eenheid van het boek* (Utrecht: Faculteit der Godgeleerdheid).
1982/83 'The Two Neo-Assyrian Documents from Gezer in their Historical Context', *JEOL* 27: 76-89.
1992 *The Fall of Samaria: An Historical and Archaeological Study* (SHANE, 2; Leiden: Brill).
1995 'Divine Wrath and the Conceptual Coherence of the Book of Nahum', *SJOT* 9: 277-96.
2006 'The Return of the Deity from Exile: Iconic or Aniconic?', in *Essays on Ancient Israel in its Near Eastern Context: A Tribute to Nadav Na'aman* (ed. Y. Amit, E. ben Zvi, I. Finkelstein and O. Lipschits; Winona Lake, IN: Eisenbrauns): 53-62.
2013 'Gottes Eifersucht als eine der Wurzeln des altisraelitischen Monotheismus', in *Gott, Götter, Götzen: XIV Europäischer Kongress für Theologie* (ed. C. Schwöbel; VWGTh, 38: Gütersloh: Evangelische Verlagsanstalt): 292-303
2014 'Phoenician Snakes and a Prophetic Parallelism: An Implication for Zephaniah 1,9 of a Recent Discovery in the Egyptian Pyramid Texts', *JNSL* 40: 1-16.
2004 *Between Fear and Freedom: Essays on the Interpretation of Jeremiah 30–31* (OTS, 51; Leiden: Brill).
2021 *Israel's Past Seen from the Present: Studies on History and Religion in Ancient Israel and Judah* (BZAW, 535; Berlin: Walter de Gruyter).

Becking, J., D. Becking and B. Becking
2018 *Van Hoedekenskerke tot Hertensprong: Herinneringen aan Augustus Gerard Theodoor (Guus) Becking 1920–1957* (Amersfoort: Bekking & Blitz).

Beek, M.A.
1948 'The Religious Background of Amos II 6-8', in *Oudtestamentische Studiën* 5 (Leiden: Brill): 132-41.

Berlejung, A.
 2006 'Erinnerungen an Assyrien in Nahum 2,4–3,19', in *Die unwiderstehliche Wahrheit: Studien zur alttestamentlichen Prophetie: Festschrift für Arndt Meinhold* (ed. R. Lux and E.-J. Waschke; ABG, 23; Leipzig: Evangelische Verlagsanstalt): 323-56.
 2012 'The Assyrians in the West: Assyrianization, Colonialism, Indifference, or Development Policy?', in *Congress Volume Helsinki 2010* (ed. M. Nissinen; VTSup, 148; Leiden: Brill): 21-59.

Berger, P.-L.
 1970 'Zur Bedeutung des in den akkadischen Texten aus Ugarit bezeugten Ortsnamen Ḫilu (Ḫl)', *UF* 2: 340-46.

Berlin, A.
 1994 *Zephaniah: A New Translation with Introduction and Commentary* (AB, 25A; New York: Doubleday).

Berlinerblau, J.
 1996 *The Vow and the 'Popular Religious Groups' of Ancient Israel: A Philological and Sociological Inquiry* (JSOTSup, 210; Sheffield: Sheffield Academic Press.

Blaxter, M.
 1993 'Why Do the Victims Blame Themselves?', in *Worlds of Illness: Biographical and Cultural Perspectives on Health and Disease* (ed. A. Radley; London: Routledge): 136-54.

Bloch, M.
 1949 *La société féodale: La formation des liens de dépendance* (Paris: Albin Michel).

Bonatz, D.
 2004 'Ashurbanipal's Headhunt: An Anthropological Perspective', *Iraq* 66: 93-101.

Borger, R.
 1956 *Die Inschriften Asarhaddons Königs von Assyrien* (AfO Beiheft 9; Graz: Selbtsverlag).

Bosman, J.P.
 2002 'The Good, the Bad and the Belial: Traces of Wisdom in the Prophetic Rhetoric of Nahum', *OTE* 15: 589-99.

Brachmańska, M.
 2021 'What Was Eating the Harvest? Ancient Egyptian Crop Pests and their Control', in *Fierce Lions, Angry Mice and Fat-Tailed Sheep: Animal Encounters in the Ancient Near East* (ed. L. Recht and C. Tsouparopoulou; Cambridge: McDonald Institute for Archaeological Research): 147-58.

Budge, E.A.W., and L.W. King
 2005 *Annals of the Kings of Assyria: The Cuneiform Texts with Translations, Transliterations from the Original Documents* (reprint, London: Routledge).

Budka, J.
 2010 *Bestattungsbrauchtum und Friedhofsstruktur im Asasif* (Denkschriften der Gesamtakademie: Untersuchungen der Zweigstelle Kairo des Österreichischen Archäologischen Instituts, 59; Vienna: Verlag der österreichischen Akademie der Wissenschaften).

Buelens, G.
 2015 *Everything to Nothing: The Poetry of the Great War, Revolution and the Transformation of Europe* (Brooklyn: Verso Books).

Bunimovitz, S., and Z. Lederman
  2003   'The Final Destruction of Beth Shemesh and the Pax Assyriaca in the Judaean Shephelah', *Tel Aviv* 30: 3-26.
Brueggemann, W.
  1997   *Theology of the Old Testament: Testimony, Dispute, Advocacy* (Minneapolis, MN: Fortress Press).
Byron, L.
  1903   *The Complete Poetical Works of Lord Byron* (New York: Houghton Mifflin).
Carr, D.M.
  2014   *Holy Resilience: The Bible's Traumatic Origins* (New Haven, CT: Yale University Press).
Cartledge, T.W.
  1992   *Vows in the Hebrew Bible and the Ancient Near East* (JSOTSup, 147; Sheffield: Sheffield Academic Press).
Cathcart, K.J.
  1973a   *Nahum in the Light of Northwest Semitic* (BeO, 26; Rome: St. Martin's Press).
  1973b   'Treaty-Curses and the Book of Nahum', *CBQ* 35: 179-87.
Chapman, C.R.
  2004   *The Gendered Language of Warfare in the Israelite-Assyrian Encounter* (HSM, 62; Winona Lake, IN: Eisenbrauns).
Chilovi, S., and D. Wodak
  2021   'On the (In)significance of Hume's Law', *Philosophical Studies* 178: 1-21.
Christensen, D.L.
  2009   *Nahum: A New Translation with Introduction and Commentary* (AYB, 24F0; New Haven, CT: Yale University Press).
Claassens, L.J.
  2021   'The Ethical Obligation to Disrupt: Facing the Bloody City in Nah 3:1-7', *OTE* 34: 835-48.
Clay, A.T.
  1923   *Babylonian Records in the Library of J. Pierpont Morgan*, vol. 4 (New Haven, CT: Yale University Press).
Clines, D.J.A.
  2015   'Misapprehensions, Ancient and Modern, about Lions (Nahum 2.13)', in *Poets, Prophets, and Texts in Play: Studies in Biblical Poetry and Prophecy in Honour of Francis Landy* (ed. E. Ben Zvi, C.V. Camp, D.M. Gunn, and A.W. Hughes; LHB/OTS, 597; London: Bloomsbury): 58-76.
Cogan, M.
  1974   *Imperialism and Religion: Assyria, Judah, and Israel in the Eighth and Seventh Centuries BCE* (Missoula, MT: Society of Biblical Literature and Scholars Press).
  1983   '"Ripping Open Pregnant Women" in Light of an Assyrian Analogue', *JAOS* 103: 755-57.
  1993   'Judah under Assyrian Hegemony: A Reexamination of Imperialism and Religion', *JBL* 112: 403-14.
  1995   'A Lamashtu Plaque from the Judaean Shephelah', *IEJ* 45: 155-61.
  2008   'The Assyrian Stele Fragment from Ben-Shemen', in *Treasures on Camels' Humps: Historical and Literary Studies from the Ancient Near East Presented to Israel Eph'al* (ed. D. Kahn and M. Cogan; Jerusalem: Magnes Press): 66-69.
  2021   *Under the Yoke of Ashur: The Assyrian Century in the Land of Israel* (Jerusalem: Carta).

2022 'Binding Up Samaria's Wounds: A Critical Assessment of New Assyriological Studies on the Fall of Samaria and its Aftermath', *IEJ* 72: 169-88.

Collingwood, R.G.
1994 *The Idea of History: Revised Edition with Lectures 1926–1928* (Oxford: Oxford University Press).

Collins, J.J.
2019 *What Are Biblical Values?: What the Bible Says on Key Ethical Issues* (New Haven, CT: Yale University Press).

Connan, J., A. Nissenbaum, K. Imbus, J. Zumberge and S. Macko
2006 'Asphalt in Iron Age Excavations from the Philistine Tel Miqne-Ekron City (Israel): Origin and Trade Routes', *Organic Geochemistry* 37: 1768-86.

Cook, G.D.
2016a 'Nahum and the Question of Rape', *BBR* 26: 341-52.
2016b 'Power, Mercy, and Vengeance: The Thirteen Attributes in Nahum', *JESOT* 5: 27-37.
2017a 'Ashurbanipal's Peace and the Date of Nahum', *WTJ* 79: 137-45.
2017b 'Naqia and Nineveh in Nahum: Ambiguity and the Prostitute Queen', *JBL* 136: 895-904.
2019 'Of Gods and Kings: Ashur Imagery in Nahum', *BBR* 29: 19-31.
2020 'Covenant Sin in Nahum', *JESOT* 6: 1-10.

Cooley, J.L.
2011 'Astral Religion in Ugarit and Ancient Israel', *JNES* 70: 281-87.

Cornelius, I.
1989 'The Lion in the Art of the Ancient Near East: A Study of Selected Motifs', *JNSL* 15: 53-85.

Cornwell, H.
2017 *Pax and the Politics of Peace: Republic to Principate* (Oxford: Oxford University Press).

Cortright, D.
2015 *Gandhi and Beyond: Nonviolence for a New Political Age* (London: Routledge).

Crouch, C.L.
2009 *War and Ethics in the Ancient Near East* (BZAW, 407; Berlin: de Gruyter).
2015 'On Floods and the Fall of Nineveh: A Note on the Origins of a Spurious Tradition', in *New Perspectives on Old Testament Prophecy and History: Essays in Honour of Hans M. Barstad* (ed. R.L. Thelle, T. Stordalen and M.E.J. Richardson; VTSup, 168; Leiden: Brill): 212-16.

Crüsemann, F.
1987 '"Auge um Auge . . ." (Ex 21, 24f). Zum sozialgeschichtlichen Sinn des Talionsgesetzes im Bundesbuch', *Evangelische Theologie* 47: 411-26.

Dahood, M.J.
1971 'Causal Beth and the Root NKR in Nahum 3, 4', *Biblica* 52: 395-96.

Dalley, S., and J.N. Postgate
1984 *The Tablets from Fort Shalmaneser* (Oxford: British School of Archaeology in Iraq).

Deissler, A.
1984 *Zwölf Propheten 2: Obdaja, Jona, Micha, Nahum, Habakuk* (NEB, 8; Würzburg: Echter-Verlag).

DeLapp, N.L.
2018 *Theophanic 'Type-Scenes' in the Pentateuch* (LHB/OTS, 660; London: T. & T. Clark).

Delcor, M.
1977 'Allusions à la déesse Ištar en Nahum 2,8?', *Biblica* 58: 73-83.
De Villiers, G.
2020 'Suffering in Gilgamesh', *OTE* 33: 690-705.
De Vries, S.J.
1966 'The Acrostic of Nahum in the Jerusalem Liturgy', *VT* 16: 476-81.
Dewar, B.
2021 'The Burning of Captives in the Assyrian Royal Inscriptions, and Early Neo-Assyrian Conceptions of the Other', *Studia Orientalia Electronica* 9: 67-81.
Dezső, T.
2006 'A Reconstruction of the Army of Sargon II (721–705 BC) Based on the Nimrud Horse Lists', *State Archives of Assyria Bulletin* 15: 931-40.
2012 *The Assyrian Army. I. The Structure of the Neo-Assyrian Army as Reconstructed from the Assyrian Palace Reliefs and Cuneiform Sources. 2. Cavalry and Chariotry* (Budapest: EÖTVÖS University Press).
2016 *The Assyrian Army II: Recruitment and Logistics* (Budapest: EÖTVÖS University Press).
Dietrich, W.
2016 *Nahum Habakkuk Zephaniah* (IECOT; Stuttgart: Kohlhammer Verlag).
Douglas, M.
2007 *Thinking in Circles: An Essay in Ring Composition* (New Haven, CT: Yale University Press.
Draper, C.
2015 'Two Libyan Names in a Seventh Century Sale Document from Assur', *Journal of Ancient Egyptian Interconnections* 7: 1-15.
Dubovský, P.
2006 *Hezekiah and the Assyrian Spies: Reconstruction of the Neo-Assyrian Intelligence Services and its Significance for 2 Kings 18–19* (Biblica et Orientalia, 49; Rome: Pontifico Istituto Biblico).
2009 'Ripping Open Pregnant Arab Women: Reliefs in Room L of Ashurbanipal's North Palace', *Orientalia* 78: 394-419.
Eastman, A.L., D.A. Rosenbaum and E. Thal
2008 *The Parkland Trauma Handbook E-Book: Mobile Medicine Series* (Philadelphia: Mosby Elsevier).
Egol, K.A., K.J. Koval and J.D. Zuckerman
2010 *Handbook of Fractures* (Philadelphia: Lippincott Williams & Wilkins).
Eide, T. et al. (eds.)
1994 *Fontes Historiae Nubiorum. Textual Sources of the History of the Middle Nile Region between the Eighth Century BC and the Sixth Century AD.* I : *From the Eighth to the Mid-Fifth Century* (Bergen: Klassisk Institutt, Universitetet i Bergen).
Elat, M.
1978 'The Economic Relations of the Neo-Assyrian Empire with Egypt', *JAOS* 98: 20-34.
Elayi, J.
2022 *Tiglath-Pileser III, Founder of the Assyrian Empire* (Archaeology and Biblical Studies, 31; Atlanta, GA: SBL Press).
Elliger, K.
1951 *Das Buch der zwölf Kleinen Propheten 2: Die Propheten Nahum, Habakuk,*

Zephanja, Haggai, Sacharja, Maleachi (ATD, 25/II; 2nd edn, Göttingen: Vandenhoeck & Ruprecht).

Engstrom, C.M.A.
2004 'The Neo-Assyrians at Tell el-Hesi: A Petrographic Study of Imitation Assyrian Palace Ware', *BASOR* 333: 69-81.

Erikson, K.
1976 *Everything in its Path* (New York: Simon and Schuster).
1995 *A New Species of Trouble: The Human Experience of Modern Disasters* (New York: WW Norton).

Fabry, H.-J.
2006 *Nahum* (HThKAT, 50; Freiburg: Herder).

Fales, F.M.
1981 'New Assyrian Letters from the Kuyunjik Collection', *AfO* 27: 136-53.
2008 'On Pax Assyriaca in the Eighth-Seventh Centuries BCE and its Implications', in *Isaiah's Vision of Peace in Biblical and Modern International Relations* (ed. R. Cohen and R. Westbrook; New York: Palgrave Macmillan): 17-35.
2010 *Guerre et paix en Assyrie: Religion et impérialisme* (Paris: Publications de l'École Pratique des Hautes Études).
2017 'Phoenicia in the Neo-Assyrian Period: An Updated Overview State', *SAAB* 23: 181-295.
2022 'Political/Ideological Display or Economic Need? The Problematical Picture of the Hydraulic Networks in Seventh Century BC Assyria', in *Ancient Economies in Comparative Perspective* (ed. M. Frangipane, M. Poettinger and B. Schefold; Cham: Springer): 165-86.

Fantalkin, A., and O. Tal
2009 'Re-discovering the Iron Age Fortress at Tell Qudadi in the Context of Neo-Assyrian Imperialistic Policies', *PEQ* 141: 188-206.

Faust, A.
2008 'Settlement and Demography in Seventh-Century Judah and the Extent and Intensity of Sennacherib's Campaign', *PEQ* 140: 168-94.
2011 'The Interests of the Assyrian Empire in the West: Olive Oil Production as a Test-Case', *JESHO* 54: 62-86.
2015 'Settlement, Economy, and Demography under Assyrian Rule in the West: The Territories of the Former Kingdom of Israel as a Test Case', *JAOS* 135: 765-89.
2021 *The Neo-Assyrian Empire in the Southwest: Imperial Domination and its Consequences* (Oxford: Oxford University Press).

Faust, A., and E. Weiss
2005 'Judah, Philistia, and the Mediterranean World: Reconstructing the Economic System of the Seventh Century BCE', *BASOR* 338: 71-92.
2011 'Between Assyria and the Mediterranean World: The Prosperity of Judah and Philistia in the Seventh Century BCE in Context', in *Interweaving Worlds: Systemic Interaction in Eurasia: 7th to 1st Millennia BC* (ed. T. Wilkinson, S. Sherratt and J. Bennet; Oxford: Oxbow): 189-204.

Ferguson, R.B.
2021 'Masculinity and War', *Current Anthropology* 62: 108-20.

Finkelstein, I.
1994 'The Archaeology of the Days of Manasseh', in *Scripture and Other Artifacts: Essays on the Bible and Archaeology in Honor of Philip J. King* (ed. M.D.

Coogan, J.C. Exum and L.E. Stager; Louisville, KY: Westminster John Knox Press): 169-87.
   1995   *Living on the Fringe: The Archeology and History of the Negev, Sinai, and Neighboring Regions in Bronze and Iron Ages* (Monographs on Mediterranean Archaeology, 6; Sheffield: Sheffield Academic Press).

Finkelstein, I., Y. Gadot and D. Langgut
   2022   'The Unique Specialised Economy of Judah under Assyrian Rule and its Impact on the Material Culture of the Kingdom', *PEQ* 154: 261-79.

Finkelstein, I., and L. Singer-Avitz
   2001   'Ashdod Revisited', *Tel Aviv* 28: 231-59.

Floyd, M.H.
   1994   'The Chimerical Acrostic of Nahum 1:2-10', *JBL* 113: 421-37.

Forsberg, S.
   1995   *Near Eastern Destruction Datings as Sources for Greek and Near Eastern Iron Age Chronology: Archaeological and Historical Studies: The Cases of Samaria (722 BC) and Tarsus (696 BC)* (Uppsala: S. Academiae Ubsaliensis).

Foster, F.P.
   2022   *The Semantics of* רע (*bad*) *in Ancient and Mishnaic Hebrew* (CBETh, 106; Leuven: Peeters).

Fox, N.S.
   1995   'Clapping Hands as a Gesture of Anguish and Anger in Mesopotamia and in Israel', *JANES* 23: 49-60.

Frahm, E.
   1997   *Einleitung in die Sanherib-Inschriften* (AfO Beiheft, 26; Vienna: Institut für Orientalistik).
   2019   'The Neo-Assyrian Royal Inscriptions as Text: History, Ideology, and Intertextuality', in *Writing Neo-Assyrian History: Sources, Problems, and Approaches* (ed. G.B. Lanfranchi, R. Mattila and R. Rollinger; SAAS, 29; Helsinki: Neo-Assyrian Text Corpus Project): 139-59.

Frankenstein, S.
   1979   'The Phoenicians in the Far West: A Function of Neo-Assyrian Imperialism', in *Power and Propaganda: A Symposium on Ancient Empires* (ed. M.T. Larsen; Copenhagen: Akademie Forlage): 263-94.

Franz, M.
   2003   *Der barmherzige und gnädige Gott: Die Gnadenrede vom Sinai (Exodus 34, 6-7) und ihre Parallelen im Alten Testament und seiner Umwelt* (BWANT, 160; Stuttgart: Kohlhammer).

Frechette, C.G.
   2014   'Destroying the Internalized Perpetrator', in *Trauma and Traumatization in Individual and Collective Dimensions: Insights from Biblical Studies and Beyond* (ed. E.-M. Becker, J. Dochhorn and E.K. Holt; Studia Aarhusiana Neotestamentica, 2; Göttingen: Vandenhoeck & Rupprecht): 71-84.
   2016   'Daughter Babylon Raped and Bereaved (Isaiah 47): Symbolic Violence and Meaning-Making in Recovery from Trauma', in *Bible through the Lens of Trauma* (ed. E. Boase and C.G. Frechette; Semeia Studies, 86; Atlanta, GA: SBL Press): 67-83.

Frechette, C.G., and E. Boase
   2016   'Defining "Trauma" as a Useful Lens for Biblical Interpretation', in *Bible through the Lens of Trauma* (ed. E. Boase and C.G. Frechette; Semeia Studies, 86; Atlanta, GA: SBL Press): 1-23.

Gadd, C.J.
   1954   'Inscribed Prisms of Sargon II from Nimrud', *Iraq* 16: 173-201.

Gallagher, W.R.
   1999   *Sennacherib's Campaign to Judah* (SHCANE, 18; Leiden: Brill).

Galter, H.D.
   2022   'Warrior Kings: The Changing Facets of Heroic Kingship in Assyria', in *The King as a Nodal Point of Neo-Assyrian Identity* (ed. J. Bach and S. Fink; Kasion, 8; Münster: Zaphon): 107-27.

Garber, D.G.
   2008   'Facing Traumatizing Texts: Reading Nahum's Nationalistic Rage', *Review and Expositor* 105: 285-94.
   2015   'Trauma Theory and Biblical Studies', *Currents in Biblical Research* 14: 24-44.

George, A.R.
   2003   *The Babylonian Gilgamesh Epic: Introduction, Critical Edition and Cuneiform Texts* (Oxford: Oxford University Press).

Gerardi, P.
   1986   'Declaring War in Mesopotamia', *AfO* 33: 30-38.

Gerber, M.M., and J. Jackson
   2013   'Retribution as Revenge and Retribution as Just Deserts', *Social Justice Research* 26: 61-80.

Gitin, S.
   1989   'Tel Miqne-Ekron: A Type-Site for the Inner Coastal Plain in the Iron Age II Period', in *Recent Excavations in Israel—Studies in Iron Age Archaeology* (ed. S. Gitin and W.G. Dever; AASOR, 49; Winona Lake, IN: Eisenbrauns): 23-58.
   1995   'Tel Miqne-Ekron in the 7th Century B.C.E.: The Impact of Economic Innovation and Foreign Cultural Influences on a Neo-Assyrian Vassal City-State', in *Recent Excavations in Israel: A View to the West: Reports on Kabri, Nami, Miqne-Ekron, Dor, and Ashkelon* (ed. S. Gitin; Archaeological Institute of America Colloquia and Conference Papers, 1; Dubuque, IA: Kendall, Hunt): 61-79.
   2003   'Neo-Assyrian and Egyptian Hegemony over Ekron in the Seventh Century BCE: A Response to Lawrence E. Stager', *Eretz-Israel* 27 (Miriam and Haim Tadmor Volume): 55-61.
   2012   'Temple Complex 650 at Ekron. The Impact of Multi-Cultural Influences on Philistine Cult in the Late Iron Age', in *Temple Building and Temple Cult Architecture and Cultic Paraphernalia of Temples in the Levant (2.–1. Mill. B.C.E.)* (ed. J. Kamlah; ADPV, 41; Wiesbaden: Harrasowitz): 223-56 + Taf. 50-52.

Golani, A., and B. Sass
   1998   'Three Seventh-Century BCE Hoards of Silver Jewelry from Tel Miqne-Ekron', *BASOR* 311: 57-81.

Goldsworthy, A.
   2016   *Pax Romana* (New Haven, CT: Yale University Press).

Graybill, R.
   2021   *Texts after Terror: Rape, Sexual Violence, and the Hebrew Bible* (Oxford: Oxford University Press).

Grayson, A.K.
   1975   *Assyrian and Babylonian Chronicles* (TCS, 5; Locust Valley, NY: Augustin).

1976 *Assyrian Royal Inscriptions* (Wiesbaden: Harrassowitz).
1991 *Assyrian Rulers of the Early First Millennium BC I (1114–859 BC)* (Royal Inscriptions of Mesopotamia, Assyrian Periods 2; Toronto: University of Toronto Press).
1995 'Assyrian Rule of Conquered Territory in Ancient Western Asia', in *Civilizations of the Ancient Near East: Volume 2* (ed. J.M. Sasson and J. Baines; New York: Scribner's): 959-68.

Gudme, A.K.
2013 'Barter Deal or Friend-Making Gift? A Reconsideration of the Conditional Vow in the Hebrew Bible', in *The Gift in Antiquity* (ed. M.L. Satlow; Oxford: Wiley and Blackwell): 189-201.

Hagedorn, A.C.
2011 *Die Anderen im Spiegel: Israels Auseinandersetzung mit den Völkern in den Büchern Nahum, Zefanja, Obadja und Joel* (BZAW, 414; Berlin: Walter de Gruyter).

Hall, M., L. Shannonhouse, J. Aten, J. McMartin and E. Silverman
2020 'The Varieties of Redemptive Experiences: A Qualitative Study of Meaning-Making in Evangelical Christian Cancer Patients', *Psychology of Religion and Spirituality* 12: 13-25.

Hanley, R.C,
2017 'The Background and Purpose of Stripping the Adulteress in Hosea 2', *Journal of the Evangelical Theological Society* 60.1: 89-103.

Hartog, P.B.
2013 'Nahum 2:14 Text-Critical Notes', *VT* 63: 546-54.

Haugen, E.
1950 'The Analysis of Linguistic Borrowing', *Language* 26: 210-31.

Herman, J.L.
1997 *Trauma and Recovery* (rev. edn; New York: Basic Books).

Heschel, A.J.
1962 *The Prophets* (New York: Harper & Row).

Hillers, D.R.
1964 *Treaty-Curses and the Old Testament Prophets* (BibOr, 16; Rome: Pontifical Biblical Institute).
1984 *Micah: A Commentary on the Book of the Prophet Micah* (Hermeneia; Philadelphia: Fortress Press).

Höflmayer, F.
2021 'Assyria in Egypt: How to Trace Defeat in Ancient Egyptian Sources', in *Culture of Defeat: Submission in Written Sources and the Archaeological Record* (ed. K. Streit and M. Grohmann; Gorgias Studies in the Ancient Near East; Piscataway, NJ: Gorgias Press): 189-227.

Holloway, S.W.
2002 *Aššur Is King! Aššur Is King! Religion in the Exercise of Power in the Neo-Assyrian Empire* (CHANE, 10; Leiden: Brill).

Horne, J., and A. Kramer
2002 *German Atrocities, 1914: A History of Denial* (New Haven, CT: Yale University Press).

Horowitz, W., and T. Oshima
2006 *Cuneiform in Canaan* (Jerusalem: Israel Exploration Society).

Hoyt, J.M.
2019 'Discourse Analysis of Prophetic Oracles', *Hebrew Studies* 60: 153-74.

Huddlestun, J.R.
    2003   'Nahum, Nineveh, and the Nile: The Description of Thebes in Nahum 3:8-9', *JNES* 62: 97-110.

Huber, M.
    2020   *Trauma und die Folgen: Trauma und Traumabehandlung, Teil 1; Überarbeitete Neuauflage* (6th edn; Paderborn: Junfermann Verlag).
    2023   *Wege der Traumabehandlung: Trauma und Traumabehandlung, Teil 2; Überarbeitete Neuauflage* (6th edn; Paderborn. Junfermann Verlag).

Humbert, P.
    1926   'Essai d'analyse de Nahoum 1 2–2 3', *ZAW* 44: 266-80.
    1933   'Die Herausforderungsformel "*hinnenî êlékâ*"', *ZAW* 51: 101-108.

Hunt, A.M.W.
    2015   *Palace Ware across the Neo-Assyrian Imperial Landscape* (CHANE, 78; Leiden: Brill).

Hurowitz, V.A.
    1993   'Joel's Locust Plague in Light of Sargon II's Hymn to Nanaya', *JBL* 112: 597-603.

Jacobs, S.
    2021   'Perfections of Justice? Measure for Measure Aspirations in Biblical and Cuneiform Sources', in *Law and (Dis)Order in the Ancient Near East: Proceedings of the 59th Rencontre Assyriologique Internationale Held at Ghent, Belgium, 15–19 July 2013* (ed. K. de Graeff and A. Goddeeris; University Park, PA: Eisenbrauns): 144-52.

Jacobsen, M.H., and A. Petersen
    2022   'Self-Blame: The Torments of Internalised Guilt, Regret, Shame and Blame', in *Emotions in Culture and Everyday Life: Conceptual, Theoretical and Empirical Explorations* (ed. M.H. Jacobsen; London: Routledge): 63-80.

Janzen, W.
    1972   *Mourning Cry and Woe Oracle* (BZAW, 125; Berlin: Walter de Gruyter).

Jenei, P.
    2019   'Subjugating and Exploiting the Second-Class Population of the Ancient Israelite State: The Case of Forced Labour (מס) in Light of the Population Economy of Ancient Israel', *JNSL* 45: 57-72.

Jeremias, J.
    1965   *Theophanie: Die Geschichte einer alttestamentlichen Gattung* (WMANT, 10; Neukirchen-Vluyn: Neukirchener Verlag).
    1970   *Kultprophetie und Gerichtsverkündigung in der späten Königszeit* (WMANT, 35; Neukirchen-Vluyn: Neukirchener Verlag).
    2009   *Der Zorn Gottes im Alten Testament: Das biblische Israel zwischen Verwerfung und Erwählung* (BiThSt, 104; Neukirchen-Vluyn: Neukirchener Verlag).
    2015   *Theologie des Alten Testaments* (Göttingen: Vandenhoeck & Ruprecht).
    2018   'Ein neues Gottesbild: Die programmatische Eröffnung des Buches Nahum', *ZAW* 130: 217-34.
    2019   *Nahum* (BKAT, XIV/5,1; Göttingen: Vandenhoeck & Ruprecht).

Johnston, G.H.
    2001a   'Nahum's Rhetorical Allusions to the Neo-Assyrian Lion Motif', *Bibliotheca Sacra* 158: 287-307.
    2001b   'Nahum's Rhetorical Allusions to Neo-Assyrian Treaty Curses', *Bibliotheca Sacra* 158; 415-36.

2002 'Nahum's Rhetorical Allusions to Neo-Assyrian Conquest Metaphors', *Bibliotheca Sacra* 159: 21-45.

Kahn, D.
2006 'The Assyrian Invasions of Egypt (673-663 BC) and the Final Expulsion of the Kushites', *Studien zur altägyptischen Kultur* 34: 251-67.

Karlsson, M.
2018 'Egypt and Kush in Neo-Assyrian State Letters and Documents', *SAAB* 24: 37-61.

Keel, O.
1977 *Jahwe-Visionen und Siegelkunst: eine neue Deutung der Majestätsschilderungen in Jes 6, Ez 1 und 10 und Sach 4* (SBS, 84/85; Stuttgart: Verlag Katholisches Bibelwerk).

Keel, O., and C. Uehlinger
1992 *Göttinnen, Götter und Gottessymbole: Neue Erkenntnisse zur Religionsgeschichte Kanaans aufgrund bislang unerschlossener Quellen* (Quaestiones Disputatae, 134; Freiburg: Herder).

Keller, C.A.
1972 'Die theologische Bewältigung der geschichtlichen Wirklichkeit in der Prophetie Nahums', *VT* 22: 399-419.

Kenyon, K.M.
1971 *Royal Cities of the Old Testament* (New York: Schocken Books).

Kerekes, M.
2011 'The Assyrian Provincial Administration', in ΑΠΑΡΧΑΙ, *Lectures held at the 6th conference of Collegium Hungaricum Societatis Europaeae Studiosorum Philologiae Classicae 28–29 May 2011* (Budapest: Collegium Hungaricum Societatis Europaeae Studiosorum Philologiae Classicae): 104-109.

Kertai, D.
2018 'The Assyrian Influence on the Architecture of Hospitality in the Southern Levant', in *The Southern Levant under Assyrian Domination* (ed. S.A. Aster and A. Faust; Winona Lake, IN: Eisenbrauns): 139-61.

Klopper, F.
2003 '"Nineveh Is in Ruins—Who Will Grieve for Her?" The Case of a Ravished City in Nahum 3:4-7', *OTE* 16: 615-23.

Kolk, B. van der
2014 *The Body Keeps the Score: Brain, Mind, and Body in the Healing of Trauma* (New York: Viking Press).

Knauf, E.A.
1995 'Edom: The Social and Economic History', in *You Shall Not Abhor an Edomite for He Is your Brother* (ed. D.V. Edelman; Atlanta, GA: Scholars Press): 93-117.

Kramer, S.N.
1940 *Lamentation over the Destruction of Ur* (AsSt, 12; Chicago: University of Chicago Press).

Kraus, H.J.
1973 *Psalmen* (BK, XV,2; 4th edn; Neukirchen-Vluyn: Neukirchener Verlag).

Kraus, F.R.
1976 'Akkadische Wörter und Ausdrücke, X-XI', *RA* 70: 165-79.

Kruger, P.A.
2014 'Women and War Brutalities', *OTE* 27: 147-76.

Kulick, O.
   2022   'Gender and Violence in Ukraine: Changing How We Bear Witness to War', *Canadian Slavonic Papers* 64: 190-206.

Kuhrt, A.
   1995   *The Ancient Near East, c. 3000–330 BC* (London: Routledge).

Kwilecki, S.
   2004   'Religion and Coping: A Contribution from Religious Studies', *Journal for the Scientific Study of Religion* 43: 477-89.

Labuschagne, C.J.
   1966   'The Emphasizing Particle GAM and its Connotations', in *Studia Biblica et Semitica: Theodore Christiano Vriezen, qui Munere Professoris Theologiae per XXV Annos Functus est, ab Amicis, Collegis, Discipulis Dedicata* (ed. W.C. van Unnik and A.S. van der Woude; Wageningen: Veenman): 193-203.

Lambert, W.G., and A.R. Millard
   1969   *Atra-Ḫasīs: The Babylonian Story of the Flood* (Oxford: Oxford University Press).

Lane, N.C.
   2010   *The Compassionate, but Punishing God: A Canonical Analysis of Exodus 34:6-7* (Eugene, OR: Wipf & Stock).

Lanfranchi, G.B.
   2009   'A Happy Son of the King of Assyria: Warikas and the Çineköy Bilingual (Cilicia)', in *Of God(s), Trees, Kings, and Scholars: Neo-Assyrian and Related Studies in Honour of Simo Parpola* (ed. M. Luukko, S. Svärd and R. Mattila; Studia Orientalia, 106; Helsinki: Finnish Oriental Society): 127-50.

Lanner, L.
   2006   *Who Will Lament Her?: The Feminine and the Fantastic in the Book of Nahum* (LHB/OTS, 434; New York: T. & T. Clark).

Lauinger, J.
   2012   'Esarhaddon's Succession Treaty at Tell Tayinat: Text and Commentary', *JCS* 64: 87-123.

Lazarus, R.S., and S. Folkman
   1984   *Stress, Appraisal, and Coping* (New York: Springer Publishing Company).

Leichty, E.
   2011   *The Royal Inscriptions of Esarhaddon, King of Assyria (680–669 BC)* (RINAP, 4; Winona Lake, IN: Eisenbrauns).

Lemaire, A., and J.-M. Durand
   1984   *Les inscriptions araméennes de Sfiré et l'Assyrie de Shamshi-Ilu* (Hautes Études Orientales, 20; Paris Librairie Droz).

Lemos, T.M.
   2006   'Shame and Mutilation of Enemies in the Hebrew Bible', *JBL* 125: 225-41.

Levin, C.
   2012   'Integrativer Monotheismus im Alten Testament', *Zeitschrift für Theologie und Kirche* 109: 153-75.

Liem, R.
   2007   'Silencing Historical Trauma: The Politics and Psychology of Memory and Voice', *Peace and Conflict: Journal of Peace Psychology* 13: 153-74.

Liverani, M.
   2021   'Kingship Ideology in Assyria and Israel', in *Historiography, Ideology and Politics in the Ancient Near East and Israel* (ed. N.P. Lemche and E. Pfoh; London: Routledge): 155-67.

Loewenstamm, S.E.
 1980 'The Trembling of Nature during the Theophany', in *Comparative Studies in Biblical and Ancient Oriental Literatures* (ed. S.E. Loewenstamm; AOAT, 204; Neukirchen-Vluyn: Neukirchener Verlag): 173-89.

Loon, H. van
 2018 *Metaphors in the Discussion on Suffering in Job 3–31* (BIS, 165; Leiden: Brill).

Lorenz, C.
 1997 *Konstruktion der Vergangenheit: eine Einführung in die Geschichtstheorie* (Vienna: Böhlau Verlag).

Luckenbill, D.D.
 1924 *The Annals of Sennacherib* (OIP, 2; Chicago: University of Chicago Press).

MacGinnis, J.D.A.
 1988 'Ctesias and the Fall of Nineveh', *Illinois Classical Studies* 13: 37-42.

Machinist, P.
 1983 'Assyria and its Image in the First Isaiah', *JAOS* 103: 719-37.
 1997 'The Fall of Assyria in Comparative Ancient Perspective', in *Assyria 1995* (ed. S. Parpola and R.M. Whiting; Helsinki: Neo-Assyrian Text Project): 179-95.
 2018 'Nahum as Prophet and as Prophetic Book. Some Reconsiderations', in *The Book of the Twelve Prophets: Minor Prophets, Major Theologies* (ed. H.-J. Fabry; CBETh, 295; Leuven: Peeters): 113-42.

Magdalene, F.R.
 1995 'Ancient Near Eastern Treaty-Curses and the Ultimate Texts of Terror: A Study of the Language of Divine Sexual Abuse in the Prophetic Corpus', in *A Feminist Companion to the Latter Prophets* (ed. A. Brenner; Feminist Companion to the Bible, 8; Sheffield: Sheffield Academic Press): 326-52.

Maeir, A.M., E.L. Welch and M. Eniukhina
 2021 'A Note on Olive Oil Production in Iron Age Philistia: Pressing the Consensus', *PEQ* 153: 129-44.

Maier, W.A.
 1959 *The Book of Nahum: A Commentary* (St. Louis, MO: Concordia Publishing House).

Mankowski, P.V.
 2000 *Akkadian Loanwords in Biblical Hebrew* (HSM, 47; Winona Lake, IN: Eisenbrauns).

Marcus, J.
 2023 'The Enigma of the Antitheses', *New Testament Studies* 69: 121-37.

Maré, L., and J. Serfontein
 2009 'The Violent, Rhetorical-Ideological God of Nahum', *OTE* 22: 175-85.

Master, D.M.
 2003 'Trade and Politics: Ashkelon's Balancing Act in the Seventh Century BCE', *BASOR* 330: 47-64.

Matarese, C.
 2021 *Deportationen im Perserreich in teispidisch-achaimenidischer Zeit* (CeO, 27; Wiesbaden: Harrassowitz Verlag).

Matras, Y.
 2020 *Language Contact* (2nd edn; Cambridge: Cambridge University Press).

Mattila, R.
  2018 'Tribute in the Neo-Assyrian Empire', in *Oswald Spenglers Kulturmorphologie* (ed. S. Fink, and R. Rollinger; Wiesbaden: Springer): 253-58.
May, K.
  2020 *Wintering: The Power of Rest and Retreat in Difficult Times* (London: Penguin Random House).
May, N.N.
  2022a 'מִפְּנֵי מֶלֶךְ אַשּׁוּר ...: The Imitators of the King and the Empire', in *The King as a Nodal Point of Neo-Assyrian Identity* (ed. J. Bach and S. Fink; Kasion, 8; Münster: Zaphon): 171-94.
  2022b 'The Destruction of the Assyrian Capitals', in *Writing and Re-Writing History by Destruction: Proceedings of the Annual Minerva Center RIAB Conference, Leipzig, 2018 Research on Israel and Aram in Biblical Times III* (ed. A. Berlejung, A.M. Maier and T.M. Oshima; ORA, 45; Tübingen: Mohr Siebeck): 231-57.
McKay, J.W.
  1973 *Religion in Judah under the Assyrians 732–609 BC* (SBTh, 46; London: SCM Press).
Meese, D.A., A.J. Gow, P. Grootes, P.A. Mayewski, M.Ram, M.Stuiver, K.C. Taylor, and E.D. Waddington
  1994 'The Accumulation Record from the GISP2 Core as an Indicator of Climate Change Throughout the Holocene', *Science* 266: 1680-82.
Mendelsohn, I.
  1962 'On Corvée Labor in Ancient Canaan and Israel', *BASOR* 167: 31-35.
Mettinger, T.N.D.
  1995 *No Graven Image? Israelite Aniconism in its Ancient Near Eastern Context* (CB OT, 42; Stockholm: Almquist and Wiksell).
Mieroop, M. van de
  2003 'Revenge, Assyrian Style', *Past & Present* 179: 3-23.
  2007 *A History of the Ancient Near East, ca. 3000–323 BC* (Oxford: John Wiley & Sons).
Mihelič, J.L.
  1948 'The Concept of God in the Book of Nahum', *Interpretation* 2: 199-207.
Minear, R.H.
  1971 *Victors' Justice: Tokyo War Crimes Trial* (Princeton, NJ: Princeton University Press).
Moriconi, A., and G. Tucci
  2015 'Philistines in Transition: Assyrians and Egyptians in Tel Miqne/Ekron during the 7th century BCE', in *There and Back Again–the Crossroads II. Proceedings of an International Conference Held in Prague* (ed. J. Mynářová, P. Onderka and P. Pavúk; Prague: Charles University in Prague).
Na'aman, N.
  1987 'The Negev in the Last Century of the Kingdom of Judah', *Cathedra* 42: 4-15 (Hebrew).
  1993 'Population Changes in Palestine Following Assyrian Deportations', *Tel Aviv* 20: 104-24.
  1995 'Province System and Settlement Pattern in Southern Syria and Palestine in the Neo Assyrian Period', in *Neo-Assyrian Geography* (ed. M. Liverani; Quaderni di Geografia Storica, 5; Rome: Stampa di cura e Sargon): 103-15.

2000 'The Number of Deportees from Samaria in the Nimrud Prisms of Sargon II', *NABU* 1: 1.
2003a 'Ostracon 40 from Arad Reconsidered', in *Saxa loquentur: Studien zur Archäologie Palästinas/Israels: Festschrift für Volkmar Fritz zum 65. Geburstag* (ed. C.G. den Hertog; AOAT, 302; Münster: Ugarit-Verlag): 199-204.
2003b 'Ekron under the Assyrian and Egyptian Empires', *BASOR* 332: 81-91.
2004 'The Boundary System and Political Status of Gaza under the Assyrian Empire', *ZDPV* 120: 55-72.
2016 'Locating the Sites of Assyrian Deportees in Israel and Southern Palestine in Light of the Textual and Archaeological Evidence', in *The Provincial Archaeology of the Assyrian Empire* (ed. J. MacGinnis, D. Wicke and T. Greenfield; Cambridge: McDonald Institute for Archaeological Research): 275-82.
2019 'A Recently Unearthed Assyrian Road Station (*bīt mardīti*) near Tel Aphek', *Kaskal* 16: 133-38.

Na'aman, N., and Y. Thareani-Sussely
2006 'Dating the Appearance of Imitations of Assyrian Ware in Southern Palestine', *Tel Aviv* 33: 61-82.

Na'aman, N., and R. Zadok
2000 'Assyrian Deportations to the Province of Samerina in the Light of Two Cuneiform Tablets from Tel Hadid', *Tel Aviv* 27: 159-88.

Nelson, R.D.
1986 'The Altar of Ahaz: A Revisionist View', *HAR* 10: 267-76.

Noegel, S.B.
2021 *Wordplay in Ancient Near Eastern Texts* (ANEM, 26; Atlanta, GA: SBL Press).

Nogalski, J.L.
1993a *Literary Precursors to the Book of the Twelve* (BZAW, 217; Berlin: de Gruyter).
1993b *Redactional Processes in the Book of the Twelve* (BZAW, 218; Berlin: de Gruyter).

Novak, M., and A. Fuchs
2021 'Azatiwada, Awariku from the "House of Mopsos", and Assyria. On the Dating of Karatepe in Cilicia', in *Beyond All Boundaries. Anatolia in the 1st Millennium B.C.* (ed. A. Payne, Š. Velharticka and J. Wintjes; OBO, 295; Leuven: Peeters): 397-466.

Oates, J.
1959 'Late Assyrian Pottery from Fort Shalmaneser', *Iraq* 21: 130-46.

O'Brien, J.M.
2002 *Nahum* (Readings; London: Sheffield Academic Press).
2004 *Nahum, Habakkuk, Zephaniah, Haggai, Zechariah, Malachi* (Abingdon Old Testament Commentaries; Nashville, TN: Abingdon Press).

Oded, B.
1979 *Mass Deportations and Deportees in the Neo-Assyrian Empire* (Wiesbaden: Reichert).

Olmstead, A.T.
1931 *History of Palestine and Syria to the Macedonian Conquest* (New York: Charles Scribner).

Olyan, S.M.
   2004   *Biblical Mourning: Ritual and Social Dimensions* (Oxford: Oxford University Press).

Ornan, T., S. Ortiz, and S. Wolff
   2013   'A Newly Discovered Neo-Assyrian Cylinder Seal from Gezer in Context', *IEJ* 63: 6-25.

Otto, E.
   1994   *Theologische Ethik des Alten Testaments* (ThW, 3.2; Stuttgart: Kohlhammer).
   1999   *Krieg und Frieden in der hebräischen Bibel und im Alten Orient: Aspekte für eine Friedensordnung in der Moderne* (Theologie und Frieden, 18; Stuttgart, Berlin: Kohlhammer).

Parker, B.
   1961   'Administrative Tablets from the North-West Palace, Nimrud', *Iraq* 23: 15-67.

Parpola, S.
   2003   'Assyria's Expansion in the 8th and 7th Centuries and its Long-Term Repercussions in the West', in *Symbiosis, Symbolism, and the Power of the Past: Canaan, Ancient Israel, and their Neighbors from the Late Bronze Age through Roman Palaestina; Proceedings of the Centennial Symposium, W.F. Albright Institute of Archaeological Research and American Schools of Oriental Research, Jerusalem, May 29–31* (ed. W.G. Dever and S. Gitin; Winona Lake, IN: Eisenbrauns): 99-11.

Pearson, G.W., and M. Stuiver
   1986   'High-Precision Calibration of the Radiocarbon Time Scale, 500–2500 BC', *Radiocarbon* 28: 839-62.

Peels, H.G.L.
   1995   *The Vengeance of God: The Meaning of the Root NQM and the Function of the NQM-texts in the Context of Divine Revelation in the Old Testament* (OTS, 31; Leiden: Brill).

Petersen, D.L.
   2002   *The Prophetic Literature: An Introduction* (Louisville, KY: Westminster John Knox Press).

Pinker, A.
   2003a   'On the Meaning of *htkbd* in Nahum III 15', *VT* 53. 558-61.
   2003b   'Upon an Attack in Nahum 2:2', *JHS* 4: # 7.
   2004   'Smoking Out the Fire in Nahum II 14', *BN* 123: 45-48.
   2005   'Descent of the Goddess Ishtar to the Netherworld and Nahum II 8', *VT* 55: 89-100.
   2006   'Nahum and the Greek Tradition on Nineveh's Fall', *JHS* 6: # 8.

Portier-Young, A.E.
   2012   'Drinking the Cup of Horror and Gnawing on its Shards: Biblical Theology through Biblical Violence, Not around It', in *Beyond Biblical Theologies* (ed. H. Assel, S. Beyerle and C. Böttrich; WUNT, 297; Tübingen: Mohr Siebeck): 387-408.

Portuese, L.
   2020   'A Foucaultian View on the Modes of Governance in the Neo-Assyrian Empire: The Good Shepherd', *Göttinger Forum für Altertumswissenschaft* 23: 1-31.

Postgate, J.N.
   1974   *Taxation and Conscription in the Assyrian Empire* (Studia Pohl: Series Maior, 3; Rome: Biblical Institute Press).

Premstaller, V.M.
2003 'Prophecy Goes Hollywood: A Fresh Approach to Nah 2', *BN* 118: 46-50.
Quine, C.
2019 'Nineveh's Pretensions to Divine Power in Nahum 3:16', *VT* 69: 498-504.
Radner, K.
2007 'Abgaben an den König von Assyrien aus dem In- und Ausland', in *Geschenke und Steuern, Zölle und Tribute* (ed. H. Klinkott, S. Kubisch und R. Müller-Wollermann; CHANE, 29; Leiden: Brill): 213-30.
2018 'The "Lost Tribes of Israel" in the Context of the Resettlement Programme of the Assyrian Empire', in *The Last Days of the Kingdom of Israel* (ed. S. Hasegawa, K. Radner and C. Levin; BZAW, 511; Berlin: de Gruyter): 101-23.
Rawlinson, H.C.
1875 *The Cuneiform Inscriptions of Western Asia. Vol. IV. A Selection from the Miscellaneous Inscriptions of Assyria* (London: Bowler).
Rede, M.
2018 'The Image of Violence and the Violence of the Image: War and Ritual in Assyria (Ninth-Seventh Centuries BCE)', *Varia Historia* 34: 81-121.
Renaud, B.
1963 *Je suis un Dieu jaloux: évolution sémantique et signification théologique de qine'ah* (Lectio Divina, 360; Paris: Editions de Cerf).
1987 *Michée, Sophonie, Nahum* (Source Biliques; Paris: Gabalda).
Renz, J.
1995 *Die althebräischen Inschriften: Teil 1 Text und Kommentar* (HAE, I,1; Darmstadt: Wissenschaftliche Buchgesellschaft).
Renz, T.
2021 *The Books of Nahum, Habakkuk, and Zephaniah* (NICOT; Grand Rapids, MI: Eerdmans).
Reybrouck, D. van
2020 *Revolusi: Indonesië en het ontstaan van de moderne wereld* (Amsterdam: De Bezige Bij).
Roberts, J.J.M.
1991 *Nahum, Habakkuk, and Zephaniah: A Commentary* (OTL; Louisville, KY: Westminster John Knox Press).
Rogers, R.
2008 *Clinical Assessment of Malingering and Deception* (3rd edn; New York: Guilford).
Rudolph, W.
1975 *Micha, Nahum, Habakuk, Zephanja* (KAT, 13.3; Gütersloh: Gerd Mohn).
Ruwe, A., and U. Weise
2002 'Das Joch Assurs und *jhwhs* Joch: ein Realienbegriff und seine Metaphorisierung in neuassyrischen und alttestamentlichen Texten', *ZAbR* 8: 274-307.
Ruzicka, S.
2012 *Trouble in the West: Egypt and the Persian Empire, 525–332 BC* (Oxford: Oxford University Press).
Saggs, H.W.F.
2001 *The Nimrud Letters, 1952* (CTN, 5; London: British School of Archaeology in Iraq).

Samet, N.
2014   *The Lamentation over the Destruction of Ur* (Mesopotamian Civilizations, 18; Winona Lake, IN: Eisenbrauns).

Sano, K.
2020   *Die Deportationspraxis in neuassyrischer Zeit* (Alter Orient und Altes Testament, 466; Münster: Ugarit Verlag).

Savran, G.W.
2003   'Theophany as Type Scene', *Prooftexts* 23: 119-49.

Scaer, R.
2014   *The Body Bears the Burden: Trauma, Dissociation, and Disease* (New York: Routledge).

Schaudig, H.
2019   *Explaining Disaster: Tradition and Transformation of the 'Catastrophe of Ibbi-Sîn' in Babylonian Literature* (Münster: Zaphon).

Schneider, T.
1988   'Nahum und Theben: zum topographisch-historischen Hintergrund von Nah 3, 8f', *BN* 44: 63-73.

Schloen, D.J.
2001   *The House of the Father as Fact and Symbol: Patrimonialism in Ugarit and the Ancient Near East* (Studies in the Archaeology and History of the Levant, 2), Winona Lake, IN: Eisenbrauns.

Scoralick, R.
2002   *Gottes Güte und Gottes Zorn: die Gottesprädikationen in Ex 34,6f und ihre intertextuellen Beziehungen zum Zwölfprophetenbuch* (HBS, 33; Freiburg im Breisgau: Herder).

Schulz, H.
1973   *Das Buch Nahum* (BZAW, 129; Berlin: de Gruyter).

Schurz, G.
1997   *The Is-Ought Problem: An Investigation in Philosophical Logic* (Dordrecht: Springer Science & Business Media).

Schwab, G.
2010   *Haunting Legacies: Violent Histories and Transgenerational Trauma* (New York: Columbia University Press).

Scriba, A.
1995   *Die Geschichte des Motivkomplexes Theophanie* (FRLANT, 167; Göttingen: Vandenhoeck & Ruprecht).

Seybold, K.
1989   *Profane Prophetie: Studien zum Buch Nahum* (SBS, 135; Stuttgart: Verlag Kath. Bibelwerk).

Simon, Z.
2014   'Awarikus und Warikas: Zwei Könige von Hiyawa', *Zeitschrift für Assyriologie und vorderasiatische Archäologie* 104: 91-103.

Simpson, J.
2013   'Cognition Is Recognition: Literary Knowledge and Textual "Face"', *New Literary History* 44: 25-44.

Sjöberg, Å.W.
1975   'i n—n i n š à—g u r$_4$—r a. A Hymn to the Goddess Inanna by the e n-priestess Enheduanna', *ZA* 65: 161-253.

Snyman, S.D.
2020 'The Lion-King in Nahum 2:11-13 [Hebrew 2:12-14]', *Stellenbosch Theological Journal* 6: 379-93.
Soggin, J.A.
1985 *A History of Ancient Israel* (London: SCM).
Soloveichik, M.Y.
2003 'The Virtue of Hate', *First Things: A Monthly Journal of Religion and Public Life* 130.2: 41-47.
Spalinger, A.
1974 'Esarhaddon and Egypt: An Analysis of the First Invasion of Egypt', *Orientalia* 43:295-326.
Spieckermann, H.
1982 *Juda unter Assur in der Sargonidenzeit* (FRLANT, 129; Göttingen: Vandenhoeck und Ruprecht).
1990 'Barmherzig und gnädig ist der Herr . . .', *ZAW* 102: 1-18.
Spronk, K.
1995 'Synchronic and Diachronic Approaches to the Book of Nahum', in *Synchronic or Diachronic? A Debate on Method in Old Testament Exegesis* (ed. J.C. de Moor; OTS, 34; Leiden: Brill): 159-86.
1997 *Nahum* (HCOT; Kampen: Kok Pharos).
2018 'The Avenging God of Nahum as Comforter of the Traumatized', *Acta Theologica* 38: 237-50.
Stager, L.E.
1996 'Ashkelon and the Archaeology of Destruction: Kislev 604 BCE', *Eretz-Israel. Archaeological, Historical and Geographical Studies. Vol. 25: Joseph Aviram Volume* (ed. A. Biran, A. Ben-Tor, G. Foerster, A. Malamat and D. Ussishkin; Jerusalem: Israel Exploration Society): 61-74.
Steiner, R.C.
2011 *Early Northwest Semitic Serpent Spells in the Pyramid Texts* (HSS, 61; Winona Lake, IN: Eisenbrauns).
Steymans, H.U.
1995 *Deuteronomium 28 und die adê zur Thronfolgeregelung Asarhaddons: Segen und Fluch im Alten Orient und in Israel* (OBO, 145; Freiburg: Universitätsverlag; Göttingen: Vandenhoeck & Ruprecht).
Strawn, B.A.
2005 *What Is Stronger than a Lion?: Leonine Image and Metaphor in the Hebrew Bible and the Ancient Near East* (OBO, 212; Fribourg: Universitätsverlag; Göttingen: Vandenhoeck & Ruprecht).
Streck, M.
1916 *Assurbanipal und die letzten assyrischen Könige bis zum Untergange Ninivehs* (VAB, 7; Leipzig: Hinrichse).
Sweeney, M.A.
1992 'Concerning the Structure and Generic Character of the Book of Nahum', *ZAW* 104: 364-77.
2003 *Zephaniah: A Commentary* (Hermeneia; Minneapolis, MN: Fortress Press).
Tappy, R.E.
2001 *The Archaeology of Israelite Samaria, Volume II. The Eighth Century BCE* (HSS, 50; Winona Lake, IN: Eisenbrauns).

Tawil, H.
　1977　'A Curse concerning Crop-Consuming Insects in the Sefîre Treaty and in Akkadian: A New Interpretation', *BASOR* 225: 59-62.

Tekoğlu, R., and A. Lemaire
　2000　'La bilingue royale louvito-phénicienne de Çineköy', *Comptes rendus des séances de l'Académie des Inscriptions et Belles-Lettres* 144: 961-1007.

Tellegen-Couperus, O.E.
　1993　*A Short History of Roman Law* (London: Routledge).

Thareani, Y.
　2019　'From Expelled Refugee to Imperial Envoy: Assyria's Deportation Policy in Light of the Archaeological Evidence from Tel Dan', *Journal of Anthropological Archaeology* 54: 218-34.

Tigchelaar, E.
　2017　'Thrice Nahum 3:8-10: MT, LXX, and 4Q385a 17 ii—New Proposals', in *Sibyls, Scriptures, and Scrolls: John Collins at 70* (ed. J. Baden, H. Najman and E.J.C. Tigchelaar; JSJSup, 175; Leiden: Brill): 1265-77.

Timmer, D.C.
　2020　*Nahum: The Divine Warrior as Avenger and Deliverer* (Grand Rapids, MI: Zondervan Academic).
　2021　'"Ah, Assyria Is No More!": Retribution, Theodicy, and Hope in Nahum', in *Theodicy and Hope in the Book of the Twelve* (ed. G. Athas, B.M. Stovell, D.C. Timmer and C.M. Toffelmire; LHB/OTS, 705; London: Bloomsbury): 157-72.

Toorn, K. van der
　1985　*Sin and Sanction in Israel and Mesopotamia: A Comparative Study* (SSN, 22; Assen: van Gorcum).

Toro, B.
　2022　*The Pax Assyriaca: The Historical Evolution of Civilisations and Archaeology of Empires* (Oxford: Archaeopress Publishing).

Tuell, S.S.
　2016　*Reading Nahum–Malachi: A Literary and Theological Commentary* (Macon, GA: Smyth & Helwys).

Tuqa, J.H., et al.
　2014　'Impact of Severe Climate Variability on Lion Home Range and Movement Patterns in the Amboseli Ecosystem, Kenya', *Global Ecology and Conservation* 2: 1-10.

Uehlinger, C.
　1996　'Astralkultpriester und Fremdgekleidete, Kanaanvolk und Silberwäger: zur Verknüpfung von Kult- und Sozialkritik in Zef 1', in *Der Tag wird kommen: Ein interkontextuelles Gespräch über das Buch des Propheten Zefanja* (ed. W. Dietrich and M. Schwantes; SBS, 170; Stuttgart: Katholisches Bibelwerk): 49-83.
　2003　'Clio in a World of Pictures—Another Look at the Lachish Reliefs from Sennacherib's Southwest Palace at Nineveh', in *'Like a Bird in a Cage': The Invasion of Sennacherib in 701 BCE* (ed. L.L. Grabbe; ESHM, 4 = JSOTSup, 363; Sheffield: Academic Press): 221-305.

Unthank, K.W.
　2019　'How Self-Blame Empowers and Disempowers Survivors of Interpersonal Trauma: An Intuitive Inquiry', *Qualitative Psychology* 6: 359-78.

Ussishkin, D.
1982 *The Conquest of Lachish by Sennacherib* (PIA, 6; Tel Aviv: Institute for Archaeology).

Utley, F.
1949 *The High Cost of Vengeance* (Chicago: Henry Regnery).

Valk, J.
2020 'Crime and Punishment: Deportation in the Levant in the Age of Assyrian Hegemony', *BASOR* 384: 77-103.

Vanhoozer, K.J.
2009 *Is There a Meaning in This Text?: The Bible, the Reader, and the Morality of Literary Knowledge* (10th anniversary edn, Grand Rapids, MI: Zondervan Academic).

Vermeulen, K.
2017 'The Body of Nineveh: The Conceptual Image of the City in Nahum 2–3', *JHS* 17 (2017) # 1, DOI:10.5508/jhs.2017.v17.a1.

Volkan, V.D.
1998 *Bloodlines: From Ethnic Pride to Ethnic Terrorism* (New York: Farrar, Straus, and Giroux).

Vreugdenhil, G.C.
2020 *Psalm 91 and Demonic Menace* (OTS, 77; Leiden: Brill).

Walker, J.
2022 *The Power of Images: The Poetics of Violence in Lamentations 2 and Ancient Near Eastern Art* (OBO, 297; Leuven: Peeters).

Watanabe, C.E.
2002 *Animal Symbolism in Mesopotamia: A Contextual Approach* (Wiener Offener Orientalistik, 100; Vienna: Institut für Orientalistik d. Universität Wien).
2004 'The "Continuous Style" in the Narrative Scheme of Assurbanipal's Reliefs', *Iraq* 66: 103-14.
2021 'The King as a Fierce Lion and a Lion Hunter: The Ambivalent Relationship between the King and the Lion in Mesopotamia', in *Fierce Lions, Angry Mice and Fat-Tailed Sheep: Animal Encounters in the Ancient Near East* (ed. L. Recht and C. Tsouparopoulou; Cambridge: McDonald Institute for Archaeological Research): 113-21.

Watanabe, K.
1987 *Die adê-Vereidigung anlässlich der Thronfolgeregelung Asarhaddons* (Baghdader Mitteilungen, Beiheft, 3; Berlin: Man Verlag).

Watters, E.R., et al.
2023 'Examining the Associations between Childhood Trauma, Resilience, and Depression: A Multivariate Meta-Analysis', *Trauma, Violence, & Abuse* 24: 231-44.

Wazana, N.
2016 'Ahaz and the Altar from Damascus (2 Kings 16:10-16)', in *In Search for Aram and Israel: Politics, Culture, and Identity* (ed. O. Sergi, M. Oeming and I.J. de Hulster; ORA, 20; Tübingen: Mohr Siebeck): 379-99.

Weiten, W., and M. Lloyd
2008 *Psychology Applied to Modern Life: Adjustments in the 21st Century* (9th edn; Belmont, MA: Wadsworth Cengage Learning).

Wellhausen, J.
1963 *Die kleine Propheten übersetzt und erklärt* (4th edn; Berlin: de Gruyter).

Wenyi, J.O.
  2021   *Piles of Slain, Heaps of Corpses: Reading Prophetic Poetry and Violence in African Context* (Eugene, OR: Wipf & Stock).

Wessels, W.J.
  2014   'Subversion of Power: Exploring the Lion Metaphor in Nahum 2:12-14', *OTE* 27: 703-21.
  2018   'Cultural Sensitive Readings of Nahum 3:1-7', *HTS Theological Studies* 74: 1-7.
  2020   'A Critical Reflection on the Presentation and Reception of Yahweh as a Violent Deity in the Book of Nahum', in *Violence in the Hebrew Bible: Between Text and Reception* (ed. J. van Ruiten and K. van Bekkum; OTS, 79; Leiden: Brill): 338-57.

West, C., and D. Cronshaw
  2023   'Warrior Welcome Home: A Phenomenological Case Study of Moral Injury and Soul Repair', *Journal of Spirituality in Mental Health* 25: 177-97.

Westermann, C.
  1964   *Grundformen prophetischer Rede* (BEvTh, 31; München: Kaiser Verlag).
  1991   *Basic Forms of Prophetic Speech* (Louisville, KY: Westminster John Knox Press).

Wilson, I.D.
  2012   'Judean Pillar Figurines and Ethnic Identity in the Shadow of Assyria', *JSOT* 36: 259-78.

Winter, I.J.
  1981   'Royal Rhetoric and the Development of Historical Narrative in Neo-Assyrian Reliefs', *Studies in Visual Communication* 7: 2-38.

Wiseman, D.J.
  1958   *The Vassal-Treaties of Esarhaddon* (London: British School of Archaeology in Iraq).

Wobst, H.M.
  1977   'Stylistic Behavior and Information Exchange', in *For the Director: Research Essays in Honor of James B. Griffin* (ed. C.E. Cleland; Anthropological Papers, 61; Ann Arbor, MI: Museum of Anthropology): 317-42.

Wöhrle, J.
  2008   *Der Abschluss des Zwölfprophetenbuches: Buchübergreifende Redaktionsprozesse in den späten Sammlungen* (BZAW, 389; Berlin: Walter de Gruyter).
  2018   'Woe to the Bloody City'(Nah 3: 1): Postcolonial Perspectives on the Image of Assyria in the Book of Nahum and its Early Reception History', *Semitica* 60: 537-55.

Woody, W.C.
  2019   'Divine Injustice: *Violence and Violation as Prophetic Image of God'*, *Diakrisis Yearbook of Theology and Philosophy* 2: 9-24.

Woude, A.S. van der
  1977   'The Book of Nahum: A Letter Written in Exile', in *Instruction and Interpretation* (ed. A.S. van der Woude; OTS, 20; Leiden: Brill): 108-26.
  1978   *Jona Nahum* (POT; Nijkerk: Callenbach).

Wright, J.E., and M. Elliott
  2017   'Israel and Judah under Assyria's thumb', in *The Old Testament in Archaeology and History* (ed. E. Wright, J. Ebeling, M. Elliott and P. Flesher; Waco, TX: Baylor University Press): 433-75.

Yamada, S.
2022 'To Be Assyrian Residents: A Reflection on the Integration of the Subjugated People into the Assyrian Empire', in *The King as a Nodal Point of Neo-Assyrian Identity* (ed. J. Bach and S. Fink; Kasion, 8; Münster: Zaphon): 273-94.

Younger, K.L., Jr
2015 'The Assyrian Economic Impact on the Southern Levant in the Light of Recent Study', *IEJ* 65: 179-204.

Zawadzki, S.
1988 *The Fall of Assyria and Median-Babylonian Relations in Light of the Nabopolassar Chronicle* (Poznan: Adam Mickiewicz University Press).

Zhang, Y.
2020 'Reading the Book of Job in the Pandemic', *JBL* 139: 607-12.

Zhu, P., and Y. Zheng
2020 'Constructivist Retelling of the Epic of Gilgamesh: Implications for the COVID-19 Pandemic', *Journal of Constructivist Psychology* 34: 1-9.

Zilberg, P.
2015 'A New Edition of the Tel Keisan Cuneiform Tablet', *IEJ* 65: 90-95.
2016 'The Assyrian Empire and Judah: Royal Assyrian Archives and Other Historical Documents', in *From Sha'ar Hagolan to Shaaraim: Essays in Honor of Professor Yosef Garfinkel* (ed. S. Ganor, I. Kreimerman, K. Streit and M. Mumcuoglu; Jerusalem: Israel Exploration Society): 383-405.

Zimmern, H.
1905 *Babylonische Hymnen und Gebete in Auswahl* (Leipzig: Hinrichsche Buchhandlung).

Index of References

HEBREW BIBLE							
Genesis		*2 Samuel*		51.11	106		
6.1-7	5	17.14	7	51.36	106		
22.17	100	*1 Kings*		*Ezekiel*			
26.4	100	4–12	48	6.11	101		
		11.5, 33	26	24.8	105		
Exodus				25.14	106		
10.10	6	*2 Kings*		25.17	106		
20.5	104	2.23-24	105	30.14-16	61		
32.13	100	15.6	98				
34.6-7	57; 107-108	15.29	41	*Hosea*			
34.14	104	16.10-16	23-24	5.5	83		
		16.18	23	7.10	83		
Leviticus		17.6	38; 40-41	10.2	98		
19.18	107	17.24	43	*Joel*			
24.19	113	17.25-26	43	2.13	107		
26.14-17	105	18.4	23				
		18.9-11	42	*Amos*			
Numbers		18.11	38; 40	6.8	83		
14.18	107-108	21.10-25	97				
		23.11-14	23	*Jonah*			
Deuteronomy		25	52	4.1	7, 107		
1.10	100	*Isaiah*		*Micah*			
4.24	104	1.24	105	6.6-7	82		
5.9	104						
6.15	104	*Jeremiah*		*Nahum*			
23.21-23	82	2.10	73	1	55		
32	105	3.5	107	1.2-8	56-57; 64, 103-12		
		3.12	107	1.2-3a	57; 74; 104-109		
Joshua		5.5	73	1.2	66		
5.13-15	26	5.9	105	1.3	66		
24.19	103-104	9.8	105	1.3b-6	57; 104; 109-11		
		19.13	26	1.4	68		
Judges		30.8-9	73	1.5	66; 87		
6.5	99	46.10	106	1.6	57		
7.12	99	46.25	61	1.7-8	57; 104; 111		
19.22	6	50.15	106				
20.3	5	50.28	106				
20.12	6	51.6	106				

Index of References

Reference	Page(s)
1.8	68-69
1.9–2.3	55
1.9-14	56; 58-59; 64
1.11	82
1.12	66
1.13	72
1.14	66; 69
2.1-3	56; 59; 64; 79-83
2.1	2-3; 66; 80; 82
2.2	80
2.3	66; 81
2.4–3.19	56; 64; 75; 83-
2.4-14	56; 59; 84-91
2.4-11	93
2.4-8	60
2.4	66
2.7	66
2.8	66; 73
2.9-13	60
2.9	3
2.10	95
2.11	73
2.12-14	76-77; 86; 89
2.12	63
2.13	4
2.14	2; 60; 69; 90; 93
3.1-7	56; 59-61; 84; 91-95
3.1-4	61
3.1-3	70; 92-
3.1	4
3.4-7	116
3.4	92-93
3.5-7	61
3.5	70; 93
3.7	3; 70
3.8-19	56; 59; 61-63; 95-
3.8-13	61-63
3.8-10	96
3.8	63; 74
3.9	63
3.10	63; 71; 84
3.11-17	96
3.13	71
3.14-17c	61-63
3.14	66
3.15	71; 100
3.16-17	100
3.16	100
3.17	67
3.17d-19	61-63; 100-101
3.17d	63
3.18	67
3.19	1-2; 8; 12; 13; 15; 51; 72; 101

Zephaniah

Reference	Page(s)
1.5	26
1.8	27; 50
1.9	27
2.1-3	27

Psalms

Reference	Page(s)
2.3	73
37	6-7
38.21	6
47.2	1
58	30
72	27-29
82	30
86.15	107
91	30-31
103.8	107
103.9	107
145.8	107

Proverbs

Reference	Page(s)
22.3	7

Ezra

Reference	Page(s)
3–6	82
3.1-6	82
6.16	82

Nehemiah

Reference	Page(s)
2.10	7
9.17	107
9.23	100

1 Chronicles

Reference	Page(s)
27.23	100

PALEO-HEBREW INSCRIPTIONS

Arad-ostraca

Reference	Page(s)
40.14-15	6

Ketef Hinnom Priestly Blessings

Reference	Page(s)
2.1-7	8

Khirbet el-Qom

Reference	Page(s)
	30

PSEUDEPIGRAPHAL AND DEUTERO-CANONICAL WORKS

Jubilees

Reference	Page(s)
4.31-32	113

Judith

Reference	Page(s)
13.9	52

QUMRAN

Apocryphon of Jeremiah c^a

Reference	Page(s)
4Q385a 17 ii:8	97

UGARITIC TEXTS

KTU

Reference	Page(s)
1.3 ii:9-11	99
1.14 ii:51-111:1	99

BABYLONIAN-ASSYRIAN INSCRIPTIONS

ABL

Reference	Page(s)
632:5-6	49
633	40
1201	46

Adad Hymn

Reference	Page(s)
IV R 28:2	109

ADD

Reference	Page(s)
149	39
755	38

Index of References

Ashurbanipal
Annals
I:74   14
Prism B
iii 37'-57'   62
v:79-96   76
Rassam Cylinder
Col II:37-39   14
Wall slab Room S   90

Assurnasirpal II
Annals
I 116   34
II 1   34
II 547-550   34

Ashurnirari
Treaty with Mati'el of Arpad
rev. v:8-9   71
rev. vi:1   71

Atrachasis
J 7.2   73

Babylonian Boundary Stones
6 i 13   74

Babylonian Chronicles
I ii:5   43
I iii:38-52   84

Code of Hammurabi
195-97   113

Enuma Elish
i 122   74
ii 127   74
iii 10   74
iii 116   74
vi 163   74

Erra Epic
IV 56-58   71

Esarhaddon
Nineveh A
I:53-62   90
ii:68-70   73

iv:82-84   75
Prism D
i:1'-9'   90
Succession Treaty
11-40   22
§ 38A   72
§ 40   69
§ 45   69
§ 46   98
§ 47   68; 70-71; 94; 112
§ 52   52; 72
§ 56   69
§ 90   70
§ 96-96A   69
Treaty with Baal of Tyre
rev iv:14-15   71
Victory Stele from Sinjirli
184   74
Rev. 36-44   14

Gezer Inscriptions
    19; 24-25

Guzanu
StAT 2
53   40

Lament on Ur
411-414   119

Ludlul
I 107   73; 88

Nabonidus
BM 55467
Rev. 7-11   9

Nergal and Ereshkigal
III 7   73; 88

Samaria Assyrian Texts
    19; 48

SAA
1.10   46
1.106:6-12   38
1.110 Rev. 4-13   47
1.171:14   43
1.180:10'-12'   43
1.183:12-17   48

1.215   46
1.220   46
1.221   46
1.261   46
2.2 rev. v:8-9   71
2.2 rev vi:1   71
2.5 iv:14-15   71
2.6:11-40   22
2.6:418-A-C   72
2.6:422-24   69
2.6:435-36   69
2.6:437-39   98
2.6:440-41   68; 112
2.6:442-43   68; 71
2.6:452   70; 94
2.6:461-63   52; 72
2.6:485-86   69
2.6:612-15   70
2.6:632-36C   69
3.11   28-29
3.24:24-26   99
5.291   48-49
7.116:1-6   46
8.103:10   99
8.418:4-Rev. 2   97
10.364:12   99
11.50   47; 49
14.77   42
15.280   38-39
16.63   19; 40
17.2:18-19   19
19.6:9-14   39

Sargon II
Annals from Khorsabad
17   44
120-123   41
169   34
Beth Shemen Inscription
1-7   19-20
Cylinder Inscription
19-20   41
Display Inscription
23-25   37
24   44
24-25   44
35   34
Display Inscription from palace room XIV
6-12   32-33
15   17

Index of References

23-26	34	
44	40	

Eighth Campaign
164 100

Khorsabad Room II
55-56 34
82-83 34

Nimrud Prism
IV: 25-41 16-17; 37; 40; 44

Nimrud Texts
CTN III
99 ii:16-23 37
ND 2672:1-24 46

Shalmanassar III
Kurkh Monolith 52

Sennacherib
Oriental Institute Prism
I 9
Rassam Cylinder
55-58 44
Taylor Prism
v:56-59 99

Tell Hadidi
Cuneiform inscription 19

Tiglath Pileser III
Slab from Kalhu
21:1'-11' 37
22:1'- 7' 37

UM 29-16-229
ii 4f 71

ARAMAIC TEXTS

Elephantine
TADEA
A4.2:6 62
A4.4 62

Nerab Stele (KAI 225)
I:9-11 69

Sfire Treaty
KAI 222-224 68
I A:26 71
I A:28 69
I A:29 91
I A:44 70; 94
I C:24-15 69

PHOENICIAN INSCRIPTION

Çineköt Inscription (bilingual)
6-10 9

JEWISH AUTHOR

Flavius Josephus
War
6.9.3 52

NEW TESTAMENT

Matthew
5.38-39 114
8.26 110

Luke
8.24 110

John
21.18 36

Romans
12.14-21 114

CLASSICAL AUTHORS

Arrian
Anabasis
2.24.4-5 52

Ctesias apud Diodorus Siculus
Works
II 26:9-27:1 84-85

Lex Duodecim Tabularum 113

Procopius
The History of the Wars
III & IV 53

www.ingramcontent.com/pod-product-compliance
Lightning Source LLC
Chambersburg PA
CBHW051102230426
43667CB00013B/2406